What Others Are Saying About This Book

"It is time to speak out about the obstacles that keep nurses working in submission and patterns of codependency. It's time for nurses to stop talking amongst themselves, lamenting the sorry state of nursing. It's time to take our places at the forefront of healthcare. The way to do this is to heal ourselves and our profession. In Caregiver, Caretaker, Caryn Summers boldly addresses addictions in the health care profession. She offers alarming information with a sensitive approach, and makes it okay for helpers to finally ask for help."

—Laura Gasparis Vonfrolio, M.A., R.N., CEN, CCRN, Publisher and President of *Revolution: The Journal of Nurse Empowerment.*

"I hope this book will be used as a text in nursing schools as well as a reference for hospital administration and nursing staffs. Caryn has researched this book thoroughly. The references and bibliography are outstanding.

— Bernita McTernan, Director of Mission Services, Catholic Healthcare West Hospitals.

"You've got to read this book. If you don't see yourself in it, you're sure to see your co-worker!"

— AJ, registered nurse.

"An inspired work of art! Caryn's beautiful heart speaks to all who seek recovery. Her honesty and integrity empower all helping professionals, especially the nurses. Her personal journey demonstrates how to stretch for our goals, overcome our obstacles, and create a healthy lifestyle for ourselves and those we serve."

— Karilee Halo Shames, R.N., Ph.D., Director of NEWS (Nurse Empowerment Workshops & Services), Co-Author of *The Gift of Health,* and author of *The Nightingale Conspiracy* (coming soon).

Published by
Commune-a-Key Publishing
P O Box 507
Mount Shasta CA 96067
U.S.A.

Publisher's Cataloging in Publication
(prepared by Quality Books, Inc.)

Summers, Caryn L. (Caryn Lea)
    Caregiver, Caretaker: from dysfunctional to authentic
    service in nursing / Caryn Lea Summers.
    p. cm.
    Includes bibliographical references and index.

1. Co-dependency (Psychology) 2. Substance Dependence—
Rehabilitation. 3. Nurses. 4. Caregivers. 5. Medical care. 6.
Self-help techniques.   1. Title.

RC569.5.C63S8 1992   616.86
                                      QB192-624

For information write
Commune-A-Key Publishing, P O Box 507,
Mt. Shasta, CA 96067.

Cover design by Gaelyn & Bram Larrick,
Discover Graphics, Sebastopol, CA.
Printed by Griffin Press, Sacramento, California.

ISBN 1-881394-33-6 $16.95 Softcover

DEDICATION

To all the nurses who have died from the tragic and preventable disease of codependency and chemical dependency. May you rest in peace.

Caregiver, Caretaker

From dysfunctional
to authentic service
in nursing

Caryn Lea Summers, R.N.

ommune-a-key
PUBLISHING

CONTENTS

AUTHOR'S NOTE

This book is *not* a book that stands against the career of nursing. It is actually very pro-nursing. I believe nursing to be an essential profession and it greatly concerns me that nurses are leaving the hospitals in droves, dropping like flies, and working in a state of depression and anger. None of this is necessary.

Because 97 percent of nurses are women, I have chosen to use the pronoun *she* when I speak of any nurse throughout this book. This is not to offend or deny the many great nurses who are men, but to simplify the text.

The purpose of this book is to educate, not to counsel. I release liability or responsibility for any alleged damage caused by the information contained in this book.

ACKNOWLEDGEMENTS

I want to express my appreciation to the nurses I interviewed for their willingness to be vulnerable. Their task was not easy as they shared their experience, strength, and hope. The risk to be fallible and to speak out about this subject is an important step in recovery. May their stories touch the hearts of the reader who may exclaim, "I am not alone in this." To the following nurses, as well as to those who wish to remain anonymous, I extend my heartfelt thanks:

Ann James, Catherine Eck, Catherine Harms, Cynthia, Deborah Ashley, Elaine Pettingill. Ellen McGibbon, Ellen Whitman, Gary Splawn, Karen Ball, Karilee Shames, Kathy McKinnis. Marie Bracciole and Suzanne Riedinger

I also want to thank my partner Douglas York, who has supported me with his love and expressions of faith in my work.

Thanks to my dear friend and sister, Maggie Draper for reviewing the manuscript and making final suggestions. To Don Flynn, my friend and critical care instructor.

Another heartfelt thanks to my editor Deborah Cady. This book has benefited greatly from her sharp eye and objective point of view. My job was truly made manageable by her contributions. DC, I love you!

Thank you, Chris and Sandy Smith of National Nursing Review Board, for your support in this project.

I want to express my love to the nurses who have given me encouragement in bringing light to this difficult subject.

I am grateful to my Higher Power, for giving me the gift of wisdom obtained by the experience of death — death of ego, of disparity, and of a desperate attempt to numb the pain — which has given birth to what I have to share.

Grateful acknowledgment is made for permission to reprint excerpts from the following previously published material:

Circle of Stones, by Judith Duerk. 1989, Luramedia.
Women of Power, by Laurel King. 1989, Celestial Arts.
The Search for The Beloved, by Jean Houston. 1987, Jeremy P. Tarcher.
Enabling in the Professions, by Linda Crosby and LeClair Bissell. 1991, Johnson Institute.
How Can I Help?, by Ram Dass and Paul Gorman. 1985, Alfred A. Knopf.
When Helping You is Hurting Me, by Carmen Renee Berry. 1988, Harper & Row.
Corporate Healing, by Mary Riley.1990, Health Communications.
The Addictive Organization, by Anne Wilson Schaef and Diane Fassel. 1988, Harper & Row.
The Self-Sabotage Syndrome, by Janet Woititz. 1989, Health Communications.
I'm Dying to Take Care of You, by Candace Snow and David WIllard. 1988, Professional Counselor Books.
The Dance of Anger, by Harriet Goldhor Lerner. 1985, Harper & Row.
Perfect Daughters, by Robert Ackerman. 1989, Health Communications.
Personality Types, by Don Richard Riso. 1987, Houghton Mifflin.

INTRODUCTION

CAN WE CARE TOO MUCH?

Dreams provide us with information while we sleep. They help us to solve problems, work with attitudes, understand situations, provide encouragement. In her book *The Mystical, Magical, Marvelous World of Dreams,* Wilda Tanner writes: "Our dreams act as our inner guidance system, helping us to locate, isolate, correct, and delete the errors and ignorant beliefs which not only hinder our progress but cause most of our conflicts" (1988:5).

I recall a dream that helped me to understand one of my reasons for becoming a nurse — that by helping to heal the entire world, I could avoid my own healing. I was at a party. As I stood near the swimming pool talking to friends, a baby fell into the water. I quickly jumped in to save her, pulling her out and initiating CPR. The baby was breathing, yet I continued to give her ventilations and compressions. She would have been fine, but I refused to let her go. I wanted to save her.

As I performed CPR, I noticed that my own shadow was blocking the sunlight from the child, smothering her and preventing her from feeling the sun's warmth. I saw that I was wearing my old nursing cap, and I felt the desperation with which I continued the unnecessary rescue of this child.

Each of the symbols in the dream was significant: the sun represented the fire of my higher power, which would heal me if I exposed myself to its warmth. The water represented the waters of life, of emotions, which can be dangerous yet exciting. The nurse's cap represented my need to take care of others. The CPR symbolized my need to save people.

As I reviewed this dream, I realized that I was each of the characters: I was the child who wanted to learn how to swim even if I took in a little of the "waters of emotion." I wanted to be allowed my lessons. I was not drowning. I was protected by my higher power (the sun). It was my choice to dive in to the waters of life.

I was also the nurse, afraid of letting go, finding comfort in the security of controlling the situation. My ego was saying, "You, my child, need me for protection." As the nurse, I could not back off. I did not want my inner child to risk being hurt or drowned by the emotions that accompany life. Yet as I performed my nursing skills, I was cutting the child in myself off from her own intuition and spirit. Is this what I did with everyone I cared for? Was I "protecting" myself and all those whom I loved with smothering attempts to help them?

As I sketched the images in this dream in my journal, I found that nursing was not only my skill and my protection but also my personal prison. Many of the actions that I had previously termed as caring now appeared to me as smothering and controlling. My dream was preparing me for the next step in my recovery. For the first time, I saw the magnitude of dysfunctional service in myself and in my beloved profession.

I encourage nursing students to explore the reasons they have chosen this particular career and to enter the profession aware of potential dysfunctions. Such awareness can foster change within the system. I encourage established nurses to look at existing patterns and to heal themselves as well as the profession of nursing. Lastly, I encourage nurse administrators to consider themselves as a part of this family in need of healing.

CHAPTER ONE

DYSFUNCTIONAL NURSING SERVICE:
A PERSONAL JOURNEY

I awake in a hospital bed, feeling medicated and groggy. I know this feeling well: the sensation each morning following a difficult night, when I have needed the pills to sleep. These nights have become routine, and I have accepted my need for sleeping pills as part of my medication schedule.

I reach for my purse, knowing that I will find something to help me function, to clear the fog. Cold hard reality cramps my gut. Where am I? I am in a hospital bed — though not an ordinary hospital bed — I am in a bed in a psychiatric ward!

Who am I? I am a nurse! A registered nurse! I am Nurse _____, RN, ICU Nurse Manager! I am the one who saves lives; who is needed by patients, their families, the doctors, the nursing staff, and my own children; who is never late for work or weak of spirit.

I glance at the bed next to me and see a disheveled, anguished woman who mumbles as she tosses: "I am a book of facts and figures," she whispers to herself. "Read me and learn." My God! I remember them bringing her into the room last night, medicating her for symptoms of an acute schizophrenic episode. I noticed that her speech was tangential, just as I had learned from the nursing textbooks.

I ring for the nurse. I know she can relate to me. She'll know who I am. I say, "Excuse me ... I'm sorry to bother you ... but there has been a mistake. You see, my name is _____, RN. I am an ICU nurse supervisor. I am not supposed to be here. I'm sure I was just tired. I feel fine now." The nurse — the mirror of myself — looks down at me and calmly says, "Breakfast will be ready soon. Do you feel like showering?"

"You don't understand." I try to disguise the quiver in my voice, finding professional control, hiding my shaking hands under the damp covers. "I do not belong here." My voice lowers to a whisper. "The woman next to me is dreadfully sick." The nurse repeats trite therapeutic sayings that I have repeated to my own patients hundreds of times. "I know this is a scary time; relax and we'll take care of you. Just try us for twenty four hours. Take deep slow breaths..."

Take deep slow breaths? Surely this woman is as insane as my roommate! Get me out of here! *I* am not sick! *They* are sick! The room starts spinning. I fight for control. I must be in control! After all, I control an entire intensive care unit. I control the destiny of life by the dial on a critical care machine! What is happening here? As I struggle for control, I recognize the familiar sight of soft restraints that I have often put on the wrists of my own agitated patients to control them. Two nurses are holding my arms while a third comes at me with a needle.

What are they giving me? I must know the medication, the dose, the desired effect, the half life, the adverse effects, the antidote, the... Oh God, I'm going down... numb. No more pain. And in my medicated state, the memories come, unattached, without feelings, for review: I remember *my* ICU, *my* patients, *my* nurses. I remember Bed 3, the 34-year-old brain-dead man who had suffered a heart attack and had fallen into the snow, where he was found over an hour later. We defibrillated him — shocked him with 300 watts per second — over twenty times, fried him, and created a vegetable: heart beating but nobody home.

Bed 2 was the woman who had gone to surgery for a gastric bypass to help her lose weight. During the surgery she received a burn on her intestine, and her own feces had leaked into her peritoneum. Now she had a full-blown case of septic shock. Tubes, IVs, ventilators, and chemical warfare would not save this overweight, desperate, and pitiful woman. The other beds were a hodgepodge of car accidents, surgical cases, and pneumonias. And I was in charge of their care.

I remember my job description: "To supervise the nurses who care for the critical patients, to assure quality care, to support families, teach nurses, medicate pain, and be accountable for the unit twenty-four hours a day."

To medicate pain. Yes. If the patient in bed 3 needs 75 mg. of Demerol and the medication comes in 100-mg. doses, I am sure she can get by with just 50 mg., and I could then have the 50 mg. that are left over so that I could medicate my own pain, so that I could sleep that night without nightmares and backaches, so that I could function the next day. The following day I would need a stimulant to counterbalance the effects of all the barbiturates I had taken the previous day. I would then take amphetamines and cocaine to wake me up, improve my job performance, and help me to be hyperalert, which my job required.

It all started when I began dating the new anesthesiologist, who had unlimited access to Demerol, Valium, morphine, and pharmaceutical cocaine. We both got real sick, real fast. Whenever a patient needed to be intubated for respiratory support, we would first numb up his or her nose with liquid cocaine. The respiratory therapist, the nurse, or the doctor would pocket the remaining cocaine. The first time it was offered to me, I was shocked. I am a nurse! I don't even drink! Everybody joked about who would get the leftovers, and I began to watch how the game was played.

The cocaine came in a 5-ml. bottle of 10 percent solution. The nurse would draw up 2 ml. in a syringe for the patient and set aside the remainder in case more was needed. Sometimes she hid the drug behind the tissue box, where it would be conveniently forgotten by everyone but herself.

When the crisis was over and the patient was stabilized, the nurse (or respiratory therapist) would quietly go into the room to check the ventilator settings or to administer a medication. She would draw up the remaining cocaine into a syringe or a test tube and pocket it for future use. Sometimes she would use it to stay awake during her shift.

From the first time I tried cocaine, I understood the importance of requesting an assignment with patients who might require respiratory support. This easily accessible "medication" made all *my* pain and insecurities go away. It made me feel sharp and self-assured and able to perform my job better. It gave me a feeling of superiority, and I felt like I was totally in control. Under the influence of this medication I could be the perfect nurse — the nurse who gives higher quality care, perfect baths, the right medications, the perfect treatments; who emotionally supports the families as well as the patients; who writes perfect care plans and keeps her patients perfectly clean; who prevents infections, helps patients walk, changes sterile dressings, and lowers or raises blood pressures.

I could be the perfect nurse — the nurse who skips her own lunch to feed the patient with meningitis, who works overtime and doesn't charge the hospital budget, who comes in early and works an extra shift to help out, who knows what it is like to be needed and who loves being needed, indeed, needs to be needed. I could be that nurse, the perfect nurse who is in perfect control.

"Control. I must be in control."

But here I am — totally out of control. It wasn't until much later that I realized that my lying helpless in that hospital bed was the first step of a long recovery process that would ultimately involve a struggle with a multitude of addictions: addictions to substances, addiction to control, addiction to being needed (codependency), addiction to work, and addiction to identity — all supported by institutional cobehavior (discussed in Chapter 6). The bottom that I hit was low, so low that I ended up in congestive heart failure, weighing ninety-four pounds, and diagnosed with manic depressive psychosis. The impressive element of my story is that for one long year I worked as a supervisor of an intensive care unit, chemically dependent, never missing a day, never losing control, until the moment I found myself in the psychiatric ward.

Why had I not seen my impending slow death? Why had I not been aware of the danger I was in? What had happened to my high values? I was so busy taking care of others, identifying their illnesses, their needs, their remedies, that I could not see my own life-threatening illness.

Why had my peers not seen and confronted me on my extreme weight loss, my irritability, my trembling hands, my runny nose, and my dilated pupils? Health care professionals can easily spot those symptoms in their patients because they are looking for them. But denial — a learned behavior that functions to protect people from the painful truth — keeps them from seeing the signs in themselves or their coworkers. Denial made me sick, kept me sick, caused me to become sicker and sicker right before my own and others' eyes, and resulted in my putting off seeking help until I nearly lost my life.

My personal journey of recovery has provided much of the material for this book. In addition, I personally interviewed over thirty nurses and surveyed many others covering a wide geographic location. The women and men I contacted have worked in the nursing profession anywhere from six to thirty-six years. The nursing specialties covered include emergency room, medical/surgical, intensive and coronary care, long-term care, flight/trauma, cardiac rehabilitation, psychiatric nursing, obstetrics, labor and delivery, midwifery, out-patient surgery, pediatrics, and home health.

The nurses I interviewed worked in hospitals and institutions that varied in size from 50-bed to 1200-bed. Locations ranged from rural to university settings. Many of the nurses were currently working, some had quit nursing altogether, a few had left the nursing profession and had returned. Some of the nurses I interviewed were in recovery from chemical dependency (including alcoholism), and nearly 75 percent of the total population I interviewed could identify themselves as adult children of alcoholics.

I explored many reasons — both functional and

dysfunctional — why people go into nursing. I found a population of healers in need of healing. Here was a group of people, the majority of whom cared more for others than they did for themselves. Here were people who were more comfortable around suffering than around joy. Here was a group that was at such high risk for chemical dependency that the data show nurses to be 30 to 100 times more likely than the general population to become narcotics addicts.

As I listened to the many stories, I learned much about myself and the importance of looking beyond the denial and asking the essential questions, Why does it happen? How does an entire profession so readily ignore its own needs for the sake of "helping others"? Where, in the midst of this "selfless" service, is the help for the helper?

The road to recovery is a self-healing process, not a quick fix, but a slow and arduous road that demands — as taught in Alcoholics Anonymous — rigorous honesty, admission to powerlessness, letting go of control, and allowing a power greater than the small ego self to facilitate in the journey back to health. Recovery is offered to each of us in three small words: "Healer, heal thyself."

CHAPTER TWO

CODEPENDENCY : A NURSING DILEMMA

Why do I find myself surrounded by needy people? Why do I feel overwhelmed with everybody wanting something from me? Why, when I don't help, do I feel guilty, like I am letting people down and I am a bad person? Why do feelings of anger arise in me? *They* are making me feel guilty! *They* are using me! *They* don't appreciate me! Why, then do I try to make *them* appreciate me by controlling and manipulating?

Why do I become a victim? "See how much I help? I work so many extra shifts. I am so tired." Why do I become an offender? "Everyone here is helpless! I am sick of doing it all for you!" Why do I abuse others? Why do I then feel guilty and move into the role of the rescuer? "It's all right. I'll help out. We will be fine without extra help."

Suzanne is a critical care nurse who complains of fatigue from the double shifts she has been asked to work, stating that she is made to feel guilty if she takes her scheduled days off. But what can she do when the unit is short-staffed and they *need* her so badly? She confesses to feelings of superiority when her supervisor tells her that she is the only one who can handle the balloon-pump patient or the intracranial bleed. Besides, Suzanne explains, sometimes it is easier to do the double shift herself rather than try to teach new nurses how to operate such complex machinery.

Lately it seems as though Suzanne gets angry at the slightest irritation. Last week she harshly accused a peer of letting air bubbles go through a central line, and the next day she cornered a new staff nurse in the lounge to teach her of the dangers of laying a patient with head trauma flat in bed. She was heard criticizing loudly, "You could have killed that patient just for the sake of a bed bath!"

When she is taking care of a critical patient, Suzanne finds it difficult to accept help from less experienced nurses. She says it is because she does not trust their skills, but she admits to feeling anxious whenever anybody offers to help her.

Suzanne feels unappreciated and used, not only in her career but also in her personal life. Her husband has just started to drink again, and her 22-year-old son, whose wife has left him, has recently moved back into his parents' house. But what can Suzanne do? They all *need* her, don't they?

Suzanne is displaying characteristics that are today being ascribed to people who are referred to as codependents. Some of these characteristics, according to Melody Beattie (1987), are caretaking, low self-worth, controlling, denial, weak boundaries, anger, poor communication, and lack of trust. Beattie says that codependents may "think and feel responsible for other people... feel compelled — almost forced — to help a person solve a problem... feel insecure and guilty when somebody gives to them... find themselves attracted to needy people... overcommit themselves... feel angry, victimized, unaappreciated, and used... get artificial feelings of self-worth from helping others" (Beattie, 1987: 37-39).

Suzanne has made herself indispensable to her nursing unit by working whenever she's needed rather than supporting the training of new nurses, assigning herself to the most difficult patients rather than allowing others the experience, refusing to mentor the less experienced nurses, and esteeming herself by angry actions at the expense of her peers' self-confidence and esteem.

Suzanne is not unique. The field of nursing seems to attract people like Suzanne. Just why is it that nursing and codependency fit together so well? How does codependency affect a needed and indispensable profession such as nursing? By its very description (needed and indispensable) nursing fits the criteria for potential codependency.

Sharon Wegscheider-Cruse estimates that 83 percent of all nurses come from alcoholic families. She states, "Adult children (of alcoholics) are conditioned in youth to giving service and taking care of people.... Naturally, then, they gravitate to caretaking professions (among them) nursing" (1989: 110).

Since people from dysfunctional families were validated during childhood for their helping behaviors, it makes sense that they would bring these behaviors into their careers and thus be attracted to a profession that promotes the use of their dysfunctional skills learned in childhood. As Pia Mellody states, "codependents are often *rewarded* for the inordinate amount of people-pleasing they engage in as a result of their disease" (1989: xxiii).

WHAT IS CODEPENDENCY?

Codependency is a disease. Experts in the field of codependency such as John Bradshaw (1988) say that codependency is the most common family illness because it is what happens to anyone in any kind of dysfunctional family. Sharon Wegscheider-Cruse (1989) states that codependency is progressive and just as fatal as the disease of alcoholism. It is often the primary disease that drives a person into substance addictions (drugs, alcohol, food, nicotine) or process addictions (relationships, gambling, sex) in attempts to alleviate the person's own pain.

The word *codependent* was initially applied to someone whose life had been affected by an addict or an alcoholic; codependency was a way for such a person to cope with a difficult situation. Codependency is now believed to stem from any kind of dysfunctional childhood. Codependents receive their self-esteem by focusing on how others perceive them.

Robert Subby calls codependency "a system of inhuman rules and expectations ... passed down from generation to generation" (1984: 31). He describes codependency as a condition that develops from exposure to oppressive rules that prevent open expression of feelings and interpersonal problems (1984). It is possible that oppressive rules that prevent honest communication exist in doctor/nurse relationships. Such rules may also be present between nursing and administration.

At a 1984 AA conference in Minneapolis, Sondra Smalley defined codependency as "an exaggerated dependent pattern of learned behaviors, beliefs, and feelings that make life painful. It is dependence on people and things outside the self, along with neglect of the self to the point of having little self-identity."[*] Since a nurse's primary identity may be "Nurse _____, RN," nurses may tend to neglect themselves in order to serve others.

Wegscheider-Cruse defines codependency as a condition characterized by preoccupation and extreme dependency on another person ... or on a substance ... or on a behavior... it is a toxic relationship ... that leads to self-delusion, emotional repression and compulsive behavior that results in increased shame, low self-worth, relationship problems and medical complications" (1989: 35 - 36).

These definitions help us to understand a cunning, baffling, and powerful disease, a disease so subtle that its symptoms may be perceived as desirable qualities for work rather than signs of the disabling disorder it often becomes. The willingness to sacrifice and to suffer is considered honorable and selfless and has consequently been built into our health care systems. It is written into the job descriptions of health care professionals. It becomes a part of a nurse's performance evaluation: "Patty is always available to the unit, willing to sacrifice her days off when we need her. She is an exemplary nurse." Such willingness to sacrifice is often expected of nurses and may be a symptom of codependency.

PROFESSIONAL CODEPENDENCY

David Willard and Candace Snow, co-authors of *I'm Dying to Take Care of You*, believe that 75 percent to 90 percent of nurses bring codependency issues from their childhoods into their profession. They define codependence as "a disease induced by child abuse, that leads to self-defeating relationships with the self and others" (1989: 15). Snow and WIllard define professional codependence as "any act or behavior that shames and does not support the value, vulnerability, interdependence, level of maturity, and accountability/spirituality of a nurse, patient, or colleague" (1989, p. 141).

When a nurse constantly gives more of herself than is required for effective patient care, when she attempts to meet others' needs and neglects her own, when she feels responsible for all aspects of her patients' lives, she is exhibiting signs of codependency.

Additional earmarks of professional codependency are listed in an article in the *American Journal of Nursing* (Hall & Wray). As you read the list, you might reflect on your nursing department. Consider your own work patterns. Do any of the characteristics apply to you?

- caretaking
- perfectionism
- denial
- inability to identify, express and manage feelings
- difficulty forming and maintaining close relationships
- difficulty adjusting to change (rigidity)
- feeling responsible for, or to, others
- seeking others' approval
- feelings of powerlessness
- feeling morally superior
- feeling super-responsible or irresponsible
- difficulty setting limits
- martyrdom
- lying when telling the truth would be easier
- difficulty with authority figures

• stress-related illness.

Personality expert Don Richard Riso describes the *healthy* helper as "unselfish, disinterested, altruistic, giving unconditional love to others... empathetic, compassionate, caring, warm, concerned, encouraging, generous, and giving" (1987: 49). Sound like most of us?

Riso describes the *average* helper (somewhat codependent) as "emotionally demonstrative, gushy, full of good intentions... gets overly intimate, enveloping, and possessive: the self-sacrificial, mothering person who cannot do enough for others. Feels he or she is indispensable, but overrates his efforts in other's behalf, overbearing, patronizing" (1987: 49). Sound like many of us?

Riso also describes the *unhealthy helper* (raging codependent) as "manipulative, self-serving, instilling guilt, putting others in his debt. Self-deceptive about motives and behavior. Domineering and coercive, feels entitled to get anything he or she wants from others. The victim and martyr: feels abused, bitterly resentful and angry, resulting in hypochondria and psychosomatic problems" (1987: 49). Sound like some of us?

Although Riso does not use the word *codependent*, he describes the key motivations of the dysfunctional helper in terms that are now heard in many recovery circles, such motives as wanting to be loved, needed, and appreciated; attempting to coerce others into responding to her/him in order to esteem the self.

QUESTIONS TO PONDER

In an article entitled "Co-dependence Among Helping Professionals," Mary Murck (1990) lists some questions to help the helper identify codependent traits. You may want to ask yourself these questions to see if any apply:

1. Do you have problems at work because of someone else's behavior, either the patient or the staff?

2. Do you worry about how much someone you work with drinks, smokes, eats, or works?

3. Do you sometimes tell lies to cover up for another staff person's or a client's (patient's) behavior?

4. Do you feel unimportant or not cared for by your coworkers, boss, or employees?

5. Do you go to lunch with people you don't like, or end up eating alone?

6. Do you ever make threats such as, "If this job doesn't improve, I'm leaving?"

7. Are you secretly afraid that other people are doing a better job than you are?

8. Are you ever dishonest in an attempt to avoid unpleasantness or to avoid confronting a client (patient) or fellow staff person?

9. Do you ever volunteer to do extra tasks you don't want to do in an effort to keep another person happy or to control another's mood?

10. Do you sometimes feel as if you're walking on eggshells, fearful of saying or doing the wrong thing?

11. Do you often feel hurt or embarrassed by the behavior of a client (patient) or of another staff person?

12. Do you begin worrying on Sunday night about going to work on Monday morning?

13. Do you ever hurt others or treat them unjustly because you're angry at your supervisor?

14. Do you allow yourself to take on the moods of the people close to you?

15. Do you take responsibility for everything, thinking that if something unpleasant happens or someone hurts

you, it must be your fault?

16. Do you believe you are the reason a particular client (patient) succeeded or failed?

17. Are clients (patients) becoming more and more important to you? Are you becoming preoccupied with them?

18. If a client (patient) rejects your method of dealing with issues, do you feel angry, hurt, or rejected?

19. Are you overly sensitive to criticism of your agency? Do you take it personally?

20. Do you take on more than you can reasonably and effectively handle?

TRAITS OF CODEPENDENTS

A number of common traits are attributed to codependents, among them a need to control, feelings of guilt, low self-esteem, damaged boundaries, and denial.

Need to Control

Control is a source of security for an insecure ego. Perfectionism may mask the issue of control. Perfectionism is a need for control over the environment. It may originate from a childhood where there was no predictability. Although perfectionists believe that they can become perfect if they work hard enough, they are convinced that nothing they do is good enough.

Control, masked as perfectionism, is behind the syndrome of "they oughtta wantta." The perfectionist cannot understand why her colleagues do not want to do everything perfectly. "If it's worth doing, it's worth doing right," is part of the childhood message perfectionists received. Another part of the message is, "If *I* don't do it, it won't get done." Perfectionists wonder why the other nurses don't demand immaculate sheets on their patients' beds. They believe that the rest of the staff ought to want to be through with shift report at exactly 7:15 am!

When, because of perfectionism, a nurse becomes critical of herself, the staff, and the administration, she is enacting issues of control — a primary symptom of codependency. The codependent nurse is often in denial, refusing to admit that she has any problems, criticizing others to avoid looking at painful issues. Poor communication is a hallmark of the codependent nurse, who may complain about others in their absence, blame, and manipulate by using triangulations.

Triangulation is a dysfunctional method of communication based on Karpman's Drama Triangle. There are three roles in this triangle. The Rescuer offers help or advice when it is not needed. This may be the nurse who graciously offers to help you with your patient's bed bath. The next role is the Victim, who feels picked on or overworked. The same Rescuer nurse may sigh later during the shift, complaining about how many baths she helped with and how her back is killing her. The last role is the Persecutor, who manipulates and controls by criticizing others' actions. After playing the Rescuer and the Victim, this nurse may claim angrily, "Why doesn't Nurse _____ ever pull her own weight?" and "Nobody else ever stocks the linen closet! I will not be the only one that does it!" At that point, another nurse, feeling guilty, may approach to offer help, and the first nurse may revert back to the Victim role, crying, "I am just so tired of giving so much." The second nurse becomes the Rescuer, offering to do her bed bath. Do you see the vicious cycle?

Nurses have the ability to control their patients' total

environment. They can dictate their bedtime, bowel time, medication time, visitor time. Picture the ICU nurse with her patient in bed, his life in her hands, dependent on her for the medications in the IVs to support his life. She can "Dial-a-Pressure" with a flick of her thumb, controlling his existence. Although this nurse is truly needed and the patient is actually depending on her for his life, the situation is perfectly matched for a nurse who needs control to relieve anxieties stemming from past experiences involving feelings of powerlessness.

If a nurse makes a mistake, she may feel that she has lost control by being imperfect. How many nurses have stood in front of a medication cart, knowing they have made a dosage error, and wondering whether to write themselves up? Tracy, a nurse who is working on her control and perfectionism issues, commented: "Last week, I gave pain narcotics to a patient too soon after she had been given a sleeping pill. I later went into her room. She was totally gorked out. I wrote myself up. My supervisor told me that it happens to us all sometime, but I did not hear her consoling words because I was too busy beating myself up with a psychic club!"

Feelings of Guilt

The staffing office calls an hour after you arrive home from work exclaiming, "We had a sick call on the night shift, and you are our last hope. If you can't come, we won't have anybody to care for the patients!" Such statements foster codependent relationships, especially when the system is staffed with people who were taught, "If I don't do it, it won't get done." Carmen Renee Berry describes this message as the first side of the two-sided Messiah Trap. Side two of the Messiah Trap is a message that teaches us, "Everyone else's needs take priority over mine" (1988:6) Although these two statements seem noble, they are founded on guilt and super responsibility.

Guilt is evident in the way a nurse may request a day off. When she doesn't feel well and would like to stay home, she may call the unit and ask "What's the patient load like? Is there plenty of help? If you really need me, I'll come in, even though I don't feel well." When a nurse calls in sick, she may hope her voice sounds like she has bronchitis so that the nurse on the other end exclaims, "You sound terrible! Don't worry — get back to bed. We'll be fine."

One nurse speaks of her guilt: "I had an awful cold, and I had to go in to work just to prove to my peers that I was sick. I shouldn't have been there. I had a huge cold sore on my nose, I could barely breathe, and I sounded horrible. The unit was short-staffed that day, so I had to work because I hadn't given them time to find another nurse. I finally got to go home the last four hours of my shift, totally exhausted." Nurses may develop serious illness as the only way to give themselves permission to slow down.

Guilt may be an obstructing force among nurse managers. A manager comments: "Being supervisor, I was responsible for the needs and the care of everyone on my unit. I would go home wondering if everything would be covered, ready to feel guilty if anything went wrong."

Guilt is a vicious cycle. The staff nurse feels guilty for being ill and not able to work, the nurse asked to cover her feels guilty if she can't, the supervisor feels guilty if she can't find coverage, so she often ends up doing it herself, at times getting ill, then feeling guilty for calling in sick.

System guilt is unresolved family guilt. In the hospital

setting, it is a multifaceted problem that arises from a real dilemma: it is true that people's lives may be at stake and we cannot just walk away and say it is someone else's problem. It may not be clear when it is appropriate to say no, because "Wolf" has been cried so many times. A recovering nurse states, "I no longer feel guilty, now that I am in recovery for my codependency and other addictions. I own myself now, the hospital does not own me."

An authentic nurse knows that she is not the only person who can handle a crisis, that she is not indispensable, and that her needs are equal to those of her employing institution's.

Low Self-esteem

Codependents are often attracted into helping professions that promote the use of the dysfunctional skills learned in childhood. A person who gets her esteem by making herself indispensable is outwardly referenced rather than internally focused.

Since life has often felt like a struggle for people who become nurses, such people may believe that nursing isn't nursing unless it's a struggle. Nurses' feelings of low self-worth are fostered by perceptions that they are working in an environment that is destroying them and that they do not deserve to be happy. The hospital can support a theory that life is miserable and must be endured. Pain and suffering appear to be the norm rather than the exception for people who work around pain and suffering all day long. The struggle and suffering are familiar — even comfortable — to such people.

One nurse commented that when she was on maternity leave, she felt like she had left a war zone. Yet she grew anxious to return, confessing that she missed the intensity, the drama, and the pain. This is a distorted perception of reality: life does not have to be a struggle. Hiding out in the shadow side of nursing awaits an addiction to struggle that originates from a sense unworthiness. Nurses often feel as if they are obligated to pay something back to absolve their original sin.

Damaged Boundaries

Personal boundaries are limits that determine how far a person will go to accommodate another. Boundaries help people to take care of themselves and prevent their being abused. In a dysfunctional family, boundaries overlap and there is confusion about which problem belongs to whom. Boundaries are invaded as family members are enmeshed in each other's dramas. In the profession of nursing, intact boundaries are essential to the health and professional retention of nurses.

A person with damaged boundaries experiences an increased tolerance to inappropriate behavior, just as an alcoholic develops increased tolerance to his or her substance. In the last stages of alcoholism, the level of tolerance is reversed, and the alcoholic has little or no tolerance for the substance. When the person with damaged boundaries reaches end-stage codependency, she/he becomes intolerant of even normal human behaviors; thus, rigid boundaries replace fuzzy or nonexistent boundaries.

Nurses may initially experience boundary problems by identifying with and feeling the patient's pain or by taking home the frustrations of work. When the pain becomes too great, when the nurse can no longer stand the accumulated traumas that she has been personally feeling, end-stage codependency is imminent. The nurse may become judgemental of and cruel to the patient, not responding to the patient's real needs. Damaged boundaries will prevent accurate assessment and care of patients, first by feeling too much, then by intuiting too little. Compassion may disappear, and a hardened facade may cover the nurse's tired and pained interior.

To prevent loss of compassion, nurses must learn not to identify with pain that isn't theirs. They must learn to detach, or give the responsibility for feelings to the person the feelings belong to. Pia Mellody states, "We can always handle our own pain, and we never have to handle another's pain."[*] We are most effective as caregivers when we are centered in our own well-beingness.

Nurses must learn to say no to extra shifts when they are fatigued or have social or personal needs. By saying no, they are then free to say yes when their boundaries are intact and they are responding from authenticity. Table 1 is a checklist on boundaries. You may find it helpful for assessing your own boundaries.

TABLE 1
BOUNDARIES CHECKLIST

When you give up your boundaries you	When your boundaries are intact you
Are unclear about your preferences.	Have clear preferences and act upon them.
Do not notice unhappiness, since enduring is your concern.	Recognize when you are happy/sad.
Alter your behavior, plans, or opinions to fit the current moods or circumstances of another (live reactively).	Acknowledge moods, circumstances around you while remaining centered (live actively).

Do more and more for less and less.	Do more when that gets results.
Take as truth the most recent opinion you have heard.	Trust your own intuition while being open to others' opinions.
Live hopefully while wishing and waiting.	Live optimistically while working on change.
Are satisfied if you are coping and surviving.	Are satisfied only if you are thriving.
Let the other's minimal improvement maintain your stalemate.	Are encouraged by sincere, ongoing change for the better.
Have few hobbies because you have no attention span for self-directed activity.	Have excited interest in self-enhancing hobbies and projects.
Make exceptions for a person for things you would not tolerate in anyone else/accept alibis.	Have a personal standard, albeit flexible, that applies to everyone and asks for accountability.
Are manipulated by flattery so that you lose objectivity.	Appreciate feedback and can distinguish it from attempts to manipulate.
Try to create intimacy with a narcissist.	Relate only to partners with whom mutual love is possible.
Are so strongly affected by another that obsession results.	Are strongly affected by your partner's behavior and take it as information.
See your partner as causing your excitement.	See your partner as stimulating your excitement.
Feel hurt and victimized but not angry.	Let yourself feel anger, say "ouch," and embark upon a program of change.
Act out of compliance and compromise.	Act out of agreement and negotiation.

Do favors that you inwardly resist (cannot say no).	Only do favors you choose to do (you can say no.)
Disregard intuition in favor of wishes.	Honor intuitions and distinguish them from wishes.
Allow your partner to abuse your children or friends.	Insist others' boundaries be as safe as your own.
Mostly feel afraid and confused.	Mostly feel secure and clear.
Are enmeshed in a drama that is beyond your control.	Are always aware of choices.
Are living a life that is not yours and that seems unalterable.	Are living a life that mostly approximates what you want for yourself.
Commit yourself for as long as the other needs you to be committed (no bottom line.)	Decide how, to what extent, and how long you will be committed.
Believe you have no right to secrets.	Protect your private matters without having to lie or be surreptitious.

Source: Adapted from David Richo, "Maintaining Personal Boundaries in Relationships," *The Counselor*, Fall 1990.

DENIAL: THE MAJOR OBSTACLE

Sharon is a registered nurse who has no idea what attracted her to nursing. Her father was an alcoholic; her mother was a nurse; she has five sisters who are also nurses. When asked whether her job was stressful, she replied, "I don't think about it. I just do my job." When asked about any problems in nursing, Sharon could identify none. She declared, "I don't feel guilty. I don't feel anxiety. I am not afraid of being exposed to diseases. I don't feel a problem." The key word here is <u>feel</u>. Sharon has learned not to feel anything.

Sharon is a classic example of someone in denial. With regard to her childhood, Sharon responds, "Our situation at home was unfixable. Sure I carry the trauma, but I don't let it run my life. I am not so weak that it would affect me now. Besides, everyone has an alcoholic parent, don't they?" As a needy child growing up in a home that could not meet her needs, Sharon felt hopeless, and her feelings became frozen so she could survive the pain of not being taken care of. She has carried her sense of hopelessness into her career.

Sharon has never considered the possibility of chemical dependency as an issue in nursing, though she commented that she was taking antidepressants for depression and sleeping pills because she was having difficulty sleeping.

Denial is a primary trait of codependents. Ann Wilson Schaef states that denial is a major defense mechanism that "allows us to avoid coming to terms with what is really going on inside us and in front of our eyes". Denial keeps from our awareness information that we find uncomfortable. Schaef explains, "When we refuse to see what we see and know what we know, we participate in a dishonest system and help to perpetuate it" (1987: p. 67).

Denial functions to help a caregiver stay secure and continue in dysfunctional behavior. The nurse who denies that there is a problem in nursing may be someone who is invested in keeping the system the way it is. Sharon's perception of a good hospital is one that is stable: "The people are stable. There are not many changes, you just go along from day to day." In codependency terms, Sharon is known as the adjuster, and Sharon's denial assures her need for stability. Sharon blames any discomfort on the assertive nurse who is not willing to live with the denial.

Schaef states that "addictions function to shut off, block out, and push down those feelings that addicts believe they cannot handle: fear, anger, anxiety, panic, rage, even joy, excitement, pleasure, and contentment" (1987: 88). In our addictive culture, we emphasize controlling ourselves and our feelings. Denial is a dishonest pattern that allows us to avoid feeling pain and to remain in a dysfunctional setting by preventing movement and growth. Denied discomforts will eventually manifest as physical or emotional pain. Nurses have a tremendous amount of tension headaches, migraines, pre-ulcers, gastric pain, indigestion, back problems, leg problems, feet problems, and menstrual difficulties. Denial is a major obstacle in one's path to authenticity and empowerment.

Denial is another word for "secret." I believe the wise saying, "We are only as sick as our secrets." Although discomforts will inevitably arise when the denial is removed, the removal of denial means that health is near. Recovering people tell their stories in the hope that others will be able to relate to them. I believe that telling our secrets, becoming vulnerable, allowing our hearts to open to one another's pain, is the key to recovery.

BEYOND DENIAL: A PERSONAL STORY

I accomplished great things during my years of codependency. Before recovery, my codependency was an asset to the institutions where I worked. I drove myself to be there for everyone. I was on most committees and involved in every decision, stayed late to hold the hand of a dying patient, exhausted myself of all inner resources. Whenever I was not at the hospital, I carried a beeper giving me a feeling of being indispensable.

I had no boundaries when it came to my patients. I felt their pain to such a degree that it was as if I had curled up in their beds with them and merged into their illness and despair. I became angry at God when my patients died after I had worked hard to save them.

When I could no longer bear to feel the oceanic pain of my patients, I shut down all feeling for them. I put up the impenetrable walls of hardness and became cynical. I was no longer able to feel compassion, which I replaced with the hard, feelingless rush of adrenaline. I developed the attitude of the conqueror. The patients' diseases became my challenge, and their bodies, rather than their souls, became my focus. Families that interfered with my manipulations and control of their loved one's vital signs became a nuisance. Numbers and calculations replaced feelings.

In the ensuing years, I alternated between giving too much and then losing all of my desire to give. Pity would become cynicism when my feelings were exhausted. Yet even in my dysfunction, I caught glimpses of true compassion when I would let down my defenses, when I would allow myself to touch another's soul in authentic caring. But these experiences were few.

At times, I would give so much that I would burn out and make what is referred to as a codependent geographic, moving to another location, starting fresh in another job where *they* would not take such advantage of me. And it would start over. As a new supervisor, I would quickly make myself indispensable to staff, the doctors, the administration, the patients. I found it difficult to delegate tasks, thinking that I had to do it all so that I could maintain control.

Control was masked behind goodwill. My need for approval hid behind my constant availability. Self-righteousness was disguised as my love for teaching. As my staff put me on a pedestal, I avoided closeness, intimacy, and vulnerability.

At the time I hit my bottom I was supervisor of the ICU, member of the clinical faculty for the local college and of the ground transport team, patient care provider, inservice coordinator, educator for the heart attack patients, regional critical care instructor, auditor for ICUs in four states, and a single mom! And I was all alone. I did not have one close friend to whom I could admit my fears and my loneliness.

Even in recovery, codependency can sneak in. I experienced many relapses in the last six years of my nursing career. Although today I have recovery tools to work with, the need to be needed never leaves. When I finally left active nursing because of burnout, I suspected that something significant had held me there — that I had been wallowing for years in others' misery, that my comfort level was with the sick and the needy. I saw that I had been drawn to the struggles inherent in nursing.

Judging from the severity of my withdrawal when I left nursing, I soon found out about a very real addiction to misery: I knew nothing about how to be joyful. I was shocked to find that other people were not waiting for calamity to enter their lives. I could not relate to their joy. Laughter seemed so frivolous, so irreverent. Without my nursing career, I no longer had any tragedies to focus on.

SUBPERSONALITIES OF
CODEPENDENT BEHAVIOR

A subpersonality is a learned coping response to an unmet need, colored and developed by one's past experiences. For each subpersonality, there are different feelings, behaviors, words, habits, and beliefs. Mary Marcus, RN (1988) identified six subpersonalities that typify codependent behaviors seen in the nursing profession (see Table 2). Not only is personal growth blocked by these subpersonalities, but the healing of patients and institutions is sabotaged. The roles that nurses have taken on were learned to cope with feelings of powerlessness, fear or shame and served to meet needs until more effective tools could be learned. Not all nurses fit these roles; some nurses shift from role to role, depending on the situation; sometimes the roles overlap.

The Martyr

The *martyr* denies her personal needs, believing that she doesn't deserve to have them met. The martyr neglects her physical and emotional requirements, believing that meeting the needs of others will vicariously meet her own. The message she may have received as a child was, "If you meet the needs of your parents, if you sacrifice yourself for the family, you will receive approval."

The martyr feels used, going out of her way to serve other people. She is the nurse who covers for her coworkers during their breaks and is too busy to take breaks herself. She does not ask for help, nor does she *overtly* complain. She often communicates hardship with a well-timed sigh.

TABLE 2:
CODEPENDENCY SUBPERSONALITIES WITHIN NURSING

	MARTYR	CRITIC	NEEDY CHILD	REBEL	SAINT	FIXER
Underlying Feeling	worthlessness	superiority	hopelessness	fear	grandiosity	guilt
	resentment	isolation	vulnerablility	distrust	uniqueness	pain
Childhood Message	If you sacrifice, we will love you.	You must be the best to be noticed.	You can't do anything about it, so adapt.	You can depend only on yourself.	We love you when you are good.	t's all your fault.
Reaction (co-dependence)	victimize	compete	adapt	coerce	give selflessly	rescue
Unmet Need	approval	control	security	trust	love	peace
Authentic Self Image (Recovery)	self-love	acceptance	assurance	forgiveness	self-hood	boundaries

Source: Adapted from Mary Marcus, "Who Heals the Healer?"

The martyr is the charge nurse who says, "I know that I can handle a lot without complaining, so I give myself the most difficult patients before giving them to another nurse and having to deal with *her* unhappiness." Her identity is the helper who sacrifices for everyone else. Then she looks for a sympathetic ear to listen to how tough it is and how overworked she is. Martyrs seek out systems where they can be victimized, because this is where they are comfortable.

The Critic

The *critic* presents the dysfunctional behavior of the perfect mom: "No one is as good on the job as I am." This subpersonality attempts to control others, which is appealing for the nurse who may have come from a family where she felt she had no control. The critic achieves feelings of superiority by belittling and minimizing others. She may have received attention as a child by competing with others.

The critic is the nurse who walks into the report room at the change of shift as the reporting nurse waits, frightened and ready to defend everything she did not get done. The critic nurse finds fault with and browbeats her coworkers, resulting in feelings of failure, confusion, and inadequacy in those being criticized. She is the picky nurse who snaps at the former shift, "You mean you didn't get the IV bottles changed? The policy states that they are to be changed at 3:00!" She is the one who calls a nurse to the side — or worse, in front of others — to comment that her patient's room was left looking like a disaster area when the linen bag hasn't been emptied. To give herself esteem, the critic nurse needs to feel and look superior by putting others down.

The critic not only affects the staff but also is

damaging to the patient. She may have little tolerance for the alcoholic patient, belittling "that drunk," seeing him as a bum. She lectures patients as if they were children, getting into power struggles, turning her patients into re-creations of her own childhood family — perhaps an alcoholic father — so that she can feel in control. She is so focused on others that she does not recognize her anger as actually belonging to her.

The critic may see her supervisor and administrator as symbols of a past unavailable mother, blaming management for her woes. She may hop from job to job, but everywhere she goes, she always has the same problem with her supervisors. She may try to win the affection of a supervisor with flowers, cards, or favors. When this does not relieve her need for a loving mother, she attacks the supervisor with statements such as, "*You* never understand. *You* never are there for me!" Such notes are abusive in that they are meant to evoke guilt and pain.

The critic attacks at the slightest annoyance, judging her peers and demanding punishment: "I am sick and tired of stocking the dressing carts! Nobody ever does it but me, and it has been going on long enough! I demand that you do something about it!"

The Needy Child

The *needy child* is often hidden when at work. She is the vulnerable and frightened child who does not feel safe and so hides behind the neediness of another. She feels responsible for another's needy child, yet her own gets pushed deeper inside. She may even believe she does not have any needs or wants at all, becoming what Pia Mellody describes as needless and wantless.

The needy child is often seen as subservient, meek,

and shy. She is unable to stand up for her rights. She cannot say no and is afraid of confrontation. Her fears of abandonment or rejection prevent her from refusing an assignment that she does not feel up to, and she may resort to being a victim. She functions on the passive end of the passive/aggressive continuum, resorting to sneakiness and manipulation to get her needs met.

The needy child is what Claudia Black refers to as the adjuster (1981: 9) who continues quietly with her work, shrugging her shoulder as she goes along with all policies and changes. When growing up, the needy child may have had her needs ignored. She may have grown up in a home in which she believed that she was powerless over her environment. Hence, she is uncertain as to how to get her needs met now. A supervisor might miss clues to the pain of the needy, forgotten child who may have serious problems such as chemical dependency (including alcoholism), depression, or suicidal thoughts.

The difference between the martyr and the needy child is that the martyr uses victimization to get her needs met, whereas the needy child has lost hope of ever getting her needs met.

The Rebel

The *rebel* nurse is tough. In childhood, being tough may have been the rebel's only way to survive. As a child, the rebel learned to hide her emotions. The adult rebel has now become disguised in what Pia Mellody calls antidependency, a codependent condition that is not true independence but is actually a mask for dependency. The message is "I do not need you," when there is an underlying fear of vulnerability and a distrust in needing anyone. Unable to ask for help, the rebel alienates the people she works with. Even though she may need help with something at work, her strategy is to tough it out alone, since it is difficult for her to admit she needs help and support. She is not (or at least claims not to be) intimidated by anyone.

When feeling she is not getting attention or approval, the rebel moves the unit into "high drama," with some kind of trouble. The rebel relieves her inner anxiety by finding outer control, acting out the panic that is building inside. She feels entitled to get what she wants through dominating and coercing. The rebel nurse projects her self-hatred onto others, creating sneaky outbursts for attention. Since she is unable to express how she feels, she manipulates, causing chaos within the nursing unit or family.

Practical jokes are a method of seeking attention for the rebel, who relieves her own core of shame at the expense of the dignity of others. These jokes may be laughed at, but they actually cause great discomfort among the staff and the patients. The rebel may announce to the new doctor, "We always keep charts at the nursing station for our head nurse," knowing that all charts must be kept at the bedside. The doctor is embarrassed and shamed by his or her mistake. The staff members, fearing that they may be the subject of her next prank, chuckle uncomfortably, "That's Jane for you... always joking around."

The Saint

The *saint* relies on the outward appearance of sainthood. She focuses her spirituality externally, feeling superior when needed by others. The roots of nursing originate in sainthood, leaving little room for individual identity. Judgement comes if nurses do not act "saintly." As a child, the saint may have received approval by being the "perfect little angel."

The saint may volunteer for many committees and spend uncharted overtime hours helping the next shift get started but, unlike the martyr, does not groan. The saint does what she does not to have people feel sorry for her but to be placed on the pedestal of sainthood. She is the Susie Sunshine of nursing, always there for her coworkers, for her patients, for everyone but herself.

The self-esteem of the saint is based on the need to be needed. The saint may appear to be selfless but is actually self-absorbed. She may unconsciously enable a patient to remain sick just so she can feel needed. The saint might help the patient when he doesn't need help, such as feeding him when he is capable of feeding himself. The saint prevents the patient from reaching autonomy by taking responsiblity for meeting all his needs.

The saint is the overconcerned nurse and may actually keep her patient from becoming independent. Although her attention seems to be focused on the patient, her real focus is on her need to be needed. When the saint helps someone, she automatically places herself in the superior role while forcing the person receiving her help into the subordinate role, silently labeling the one she helps as incompetent. The helper thus obtains power and prestige when the dependent person tells her how indispensable she is. Carmen Renee Berry refers to this temptation of sainthood as the key element in the Messiah Trap (1988:36).

When asked about the reward of nursing, the saint might answer, "It is a feeling of satisfaction when *I* relieve a patient's pain" rather than "It is the feeling of satisfaction seeing the *patient* become independent." The saint claims to be the patient advocate who is constantly pleading the cause of another, even when the other is not allowed to express what his or her cause is. When insecure, she reminds herself "I am a *nurse*, and people really *need* me," which reinforces her need to be needed as a way of treating her own pain.

In her personal life, the saint attracts needy people, and needy people look to her to be their mother. The saint's need to mother may be fulfilled by substituting people for her children who are grown or for children she never had. When done in full awareness, such parenting can be beneficial since an effective parent fosters autonomy and independence in her children. A dysfunctional parent, however, fosters dependency and forces her children to remain children. The saint's lesson is in learning how *not* to be a mother to other adults.

The Fixer

The *fixer* considers death and pain to be her personal challenge. She takes full responsibility for her patient's life. Eldest daughters from dysfunctional families often develop an exaggerated sense of responsibility early in life. The fixer inwardly claims all credit when she "saves her patient" and becomes angry when a patient dies in spite of her efforts.

When the fixer sees someone in pain, she feels old discomforts, and she quickly works to remedy the other person's pain to relieve her own. Believing she is responsible for her patients' comfort, the fixer feels anxious and guilty when her patients are not comfortable. She gives medication at the first grimace of pain. The fixer is very vulnerable. Since other people's moods control her emotions, she tries to control their feelings. When they are in pain, she is in pain.

The fixer is a chronic rescuer — for the staff as well as the patients. She is able to walk onto her work unit and read everyone's moods, creating a "care plan" on how to fix everyone. The staff may complain about something trivial, such as the location of the syringes, and be surprised to find that the fixer has gone to the nurse manager with suggestions on how to remedy this "huge inconvenience to the staff." The fixer on the unit is the conflict resolver and negotiator. She assures everybody, "Your problem is my problem. I'll fix it."

The difference between the fixer and the saint is in the motive behind their actions. The saint removes others' pain so that she will be appreciated. The fixer removes others' pain so that she does not have to feel her own.

SUMMARY

Nursing is a tough job. It's even tougher for the codependent nurse, who faces the challenge of recovery from a disease that is encouraged by the very nature of the job. Because many nurses come from dysfunctional families, codependency is a natural pattern of behavior if left untreated. Wegscheider-Cruse states that "these adult children in the helping professions still suffer from their own resistance to the family illness concept. To accept that information fully would be ... admitting that the helping professionals themselves have wounds that have not healed... that even professionals themselves need help in dealing with the family issues growing out of the family illness of (addictions such as) chemical dependency" (1989: 110).

I am not suggesting that nurses must leave the field of nursing to heal and to find joy. What I am suggesting is that nurses look at their addictions and their codependency and that they bring personal recovery into their careers. Codependent patterns can be changed once they are identified. The next chapter explores possible origins to these patterns.

* Sandra Smalley. Speech to physicians at AA conference held in Minneapolis, Minn., August, 1984, on audio tape.

* From a taped series on codependency by Pia Mellody, 1990.

CHAPTER THREE

THE CHASE:
NURSING AND CHILDHOOD WOUNDS

All things that are,
Are with more spirit
chased than enjoy'd.
- Shakespeare
(The Merchant of Venice
Act II Sc. 6 line 12)

REENACTING CHILDHOOD TRAUMA

Mary has worked in a hospital labor and delivery department for most of her career as a registered nurse. She is highly skilled and well respected by her peers and by physicians. Mary has felt attracted to heartbreaking maternity cases in which new mothers give their babies up for adoption.

Mary herself was adopted as an infant, and her life has been plagued with bouts of depression and separation anxiety. For many years, she carried unresolved issues of the forced separation from her biological parents. As a maternity nurse, Mary unconsciously replayed the tragedy of her own story, watching the guilt and sorrow of countless mothers rejecting their children, identifying with the infants' helplessness and loss of control over their destiny:

> I paid special attention to the babies who were being adopted. I related to the pain and guilt of the mother who was giving her child up, as well as to the sorrow of the infant who would never be held by the one who carried her in the womb. I would feel the anger of the baby being pushed aside, yet somehow I did not relate this to my own anger and feelings of abandonment.
>
> After I entered therapy, I began to grieve the loss of my mother. I then learned to see the joy and happiness of a woman who was receiving and loving the adopted child instead of relating to the pain of the separation. At work, I was touched by an experience of connecting with a woman who was bonding with her new baby. I spent a long time just looking into the mother's eyes as she gazed at her child, then I connected with the sweet baby who was wanted. I held the baby for a long time, and I told her that I would pray for her to have a happy and loving life.
>
> When the new mother reached for her baby, I kissed the child's cheek and told the mother that I have been in her daughter's shoes, and that I hoped this child always realized how much her mother loves her to find her like she did. It was the healing of my own infant wounds. Identifying with this baby was my own rebirth.

Mary's story is an example of how people unknowingly attempt to treat past pain by recreating unhealed old injuries with the hope of gaining a sense of completion. I call this process the chase. Nurses may chase relentless memories through hospital corridors and medical offices. During the chase, they become the playwright, producer, director, and star of their own personal drama in which their patients play key roles. They write a recurrent plot around their pain, repeating the unforgettable moments of tragedy, memorizing the scripts, unaware of their reasons for doing so. They continually reach the climactic scene where the opportunity to heal presents itself, yet they cannot use it for this purpose until they become conscious of their chase.

People often repeat learned behaviors which stem from childhood wounds over and over until they realize that they are replaying their life story. To heal, they must have a sincere desire to know and a willingness to ask, and they frequently require therapy or a support group to aid them in recognizing their subtle reenactments. In the midst of acute pain, people may find the clue that will decipher their mystery.

Mary's clue was that she worked for many years in the very same hospital in which she was born. As part of her healing process, she pulled her name up on the hospital computer: "Baby Girl _____." Seeing her name in the computer helped to validate her existence. Mary has now met her biological mother and recently began looking for her father. Through the healing that has taken place, Mary is now able to explore other fields of nursing where her education can be broadened and she can feel challenged.

Nurses may use their identity as a registered nurse or

licensed vocational nurse to hide their own discomforts within their patients' symptoms. Hidden pain dictates how they live their lives. It may influence which patients codependent nurses choose to "fix." These nurses gravitate to certain patients: the patient in hepatic failure (terminal alcoholic liver disease) often attracts the nurse with the alcoholic father. The pediatric patient may attract the nurse who either felt not cared for as a child or is unable to have children. These nurses have stuffed their fear and anger inside them to survive a traumatic world. The emotions surface in their workplace (as well as in other relationships), seeking to be recognized and reconciled.

Debra also works at the same hospital that was the setting of her childhood trauma. When Debra was young, her mother was frequently ill, and Debra remembers being aroused from sleep in the middle of the night to travel the familiar route to the hospital with her alcoholic father. Debra and her sister spent many frightening nights alone in the car in the hospital parking lot, watching the sun come up, wondering what was going on inside this mysterious structure. Would they ever see their mother again? What was so wrong that their mother had to come to this impenetrable place?

Working in this same hospital from her childhood, Debra never again has to worry about or guess what goes on inside it. She can feel in control. Working the night shift, she can watch the sun rising from *inside* the building, relieving the anxiety that stems from feelings of loss of control and the fear of the unknown.

An attractive logo that appears on the front of this hospital symbolizes to Debra the same dysfunction that she grew up with: her family looked good on the outside, just like the beautiful logo, but was dreadfully sick on the inside, like the people inside the hospital:

> I have an old photograph of myself standing
> with my sister in front of that logo, waiting for my
> mother to be discharged from the hospital. I was
> never allowed into those mysterious corridors,
> and I knew that something terrible must be
> happening inside.

Debra has worked for many years on the surgical
floor that specializes in eye, nose, and throat surgery. She
cares for patients with cancer of the throat; she claims to
be plagued with repeated episodes of sore throats. It's not
surprising that the throat is the tool of verbalization and
that cancer is often a symptom of unexpressed anger or
fear.

> I never realized that I was angry until recently.
> I had a rage that wanted to come up, to be
> vocalized. Now, after time in therapy talking
> about this anger, I am able to consider leaving the
> department. I do not need to be around this
> reminder of my anger anymore.

As nurses examine their childhood traumas and
pains, they can uncover why they have chosen a
particular patient population. Their reasons may be an
unconscious attempt to open their wounds for healing.
Just as teachers may teach the subjects that they most
need to learn, healers may attempt to heal in others that
which is most in need of healing within themselves.

MOTIVES FOR BECOMING A NURSE

Sondra Ray, founding director of Loving Relationships Training, began her career as a nurse. Her father
died when she was sixteen years old, the night before her
high school graduation. In an interview for Laurel King's
book *Women of Power*, Ray reveals her motives for
becoming a nurse. She felt that she was not able to save
her father, yet she needed to understand his death. "I
wanted to know why he died, why they couldn't save
him. I wanted to know what the cause of his disease was,
and why people were getting these diseases, and why we
couldn't have permanent healing" (King, 1989:203). In
nursing, Ray found repeated exposure to death as she
chased the dying process in an attempt to come to terms
with her father's death.

Acknowledging one's own wounds is the first step in
moving beyond them. Nurses who don't acknowledge
their wounds may make geographic changes, jumping
from one discipline to the next, thinking that a change in
scenery will make them feel better. The next story
illustrates this.

Kathryn grew up in a strict, rigid family, where she
could not express her own spirituality and creativity
without feeling judged as crazy. Her mother was an
alcoholic. At a young age, Kathryn was pushed to be
perfect, to take over the role of mother, and to deny her
own sense of uniqueness and divine self:

> I was raised in a family where the saying
> "Children are to be seen and not heard" was the
> cardinal rule. I was forced into a role. Behavior or
> actions that weren't part of that role were

unacceptable. Years later as a nurse in the psychiatric ward, I would watch the patients in the padded cells who believed that they were God and think how beautiful their spiritual experiences were. They were experiencing what they felt as truth, and I watched in dismay as the psychiatrists knocked that truth out of them with drugs or behavioral therapy. I felt they were being treated unjustly, as I was when my parents tried to knock my true self out of me.

As a child, Kathryn had an uncle who incurred brain injury from a traumatic birth. The medications that he was forced to take for seizures caused symptoms of mental illness. As a little girl, Kathryn had always loved her uncle's gentleness. Her family was ashamed of his "insanity" and consequently had him committed to an insane asylum:

I felt such anger at this act of imprisonment, yet I was not allowed to express it. I began to live with a fear that I would be viewed as crazy if I showed my rage. As a psychiatric nurse, I could vicariously feel this hidden rage through my patients when they screamed and acted out their madness. I was intrigued and frightened at the same time by the freedom of expression they were given through mental illness. Yet I did not dare to express my own rage and risk being rejected. Even now when I get angry I fear that I may have tendencies toward total madness within my rage.

The nurse who feels uncomfortable with her peers may feel safe in the environment of the psychiatric ward.

She may not find the psychiatric patients intimidating, because the patients are all labeled as being crazier than the nurse. The psychiatric ward offers safety for the nurse who feels that something is wrong with her own mental health. Today Kathryn jokes about her own movement toward health, claiming, "I was really a Registered Nut!"

Kathryn's chase continued. Kathryn made her first geographic change when she quit psychiatric nursing to become a midwife, dedicated to helping mothers experience joyful home births. Kathryn herself was brought into this life by a forceps delivery. Her mother had been gassed with nitrous oxide and as a result was not able to push with the labor contractions. In therapy, Kathryn was led through a rebirthing experience, where she recalled her own birth and the pain of being trapped in the dark canal until the cold metal forceps grabbed her by the head and jerked her out. She had felt frightened and alone. Her career as a midwife had offered her a vicarious relief from anxiety and a healing opportunity from her birth trauma. Now that she is aware of this chase, she can perhaps prevent herself from falling into the trap of "fixing" her patients' pain instead of healing her own.

Yet the chase is cunning, baffling, and powerful:

> Recently I have felt the desire to retire from midwifery and to work in the field of alcoholism rehabilitation. But I am now able to see this as another attempt to heal my childhood wounds of helplessness: my mother recently died from the disease of alcoholism.

Adult children of alcoholics like Kathryn can be either the best or the most dysfunctional nurses in the field of substance abuse treatment. If they are in a recovery program, they learn to turn their experiences and firsthand knowledge into tools that will assist others in recovery. If they are in denial of their own need to heal, they may fall into the trap of trying to fix the alcoholic/addict, since they were not able to fix their alcoholic parent.

ONE-SIDED INTIMACY

Susan is a pediatric nurse who speaks with deep conviction of her constant availability to "my little ones." As she tells her professional story, her tone of voice declares an urgency to prevent these children from feeling abandoned. As she speaks, she rocks herself, hugging her legs, repeatedly crooning the words that she so often promises her patients: "It's all right. I will not leave you. I will hold you until mommy comes. Mommy loves you. I will not leave you."

Susan's faraway look reveals the need for security and intimacy for the forgotten child within herself. This is what Carmen Renee Berry refers to as one-sided intimacy (1988:68), in which the patient is made to be the only vulnerable one in the relationship. Here, the *other* is expected to disclose her feelings, while the nurse (or other helping professional) hides safely in her own projections. This keeps the nurse from feeling, and all pain is played out by the patient. Wounds are exposed and allowed to heal, but *not* the wounds of the nurse: the nurse experiences only a temporary relief from anxiety.

The danger with one-sided intimacy is that the nurse might project her own pains onto the patient, missing the unique needs of the individual she is caring for. The nurse might overmedicate someone who is not experiencing as much pain as she is projecting, or she might undermedicate a patient she judges as not having a high pain threshold like her own.

Susan is a perfect pediatric nurse, priding herself on being able to take a PMI pulse without a stethoscope, using only her touch. In fact, she has a difficult time not touching her patients, and her own desperate need for touch is obvious. Susan had a rare skin sensitivity when she was born; all skin contact and touch were excruciatingly painful. Even her own mother's breast caused burning pain around her mouth, forcing her to be fed with a bottle propped up in her crib. She wore a spica cast so that her urine would not touch her skin, further preventing her from being held by her mother.

Susan is an example of an unhealed healer. Starved for touch, Susan has recreated her primary wound. Feeling abandoned, neglected, and unloved, she projects her need for touch and security onto her patients, relieving her own anxiety at the possible expense of her patients' boundaries.

RESOLUTION THROUGH THE CHASE

My own chase began when I was fourteen years old. I had gone bowling on a Sunday afternoon with a boy who was fifteen. It was exciting exploring the world of boy/girl relationships. The boy bought me a box of chocolates, and I was impressed by this loving attention. After bowling, we walked over to his house to watch television. No one was home; I found out later that both of his parents were at a bar, a routine event for them. (My family as well as his was affected by the disease of alcoholism.)

As we sat down, the boy reached for my hand and nervously asked me to go steady. For the next twenty years, I suffered silently as I punished myself for my response. I laughed at him. I told him that I was only fourteen and that going steady was a ridiculous thought. That day's events led to the guilt that shaped my destiny and influenced my career choice.

The boy committed suicide that afternoon in my presence. He shot himself in the heart. I watched, terrified and helpless, as he died in front of me. Because I had no idea what to do, how to control the bleeding, how to perform CPR, or how to stop his imminent death, I simply ran outside, screaming for help. I was overwhelmed by feelings of guilt and felt powerless as I watched in horror as the ambulance drove away. I had no idea of the implications of this traumatic event when it happened, nor was I to understand until many years later why I was driven to become a critical care nurse.

I remember my silent vow at the time to never hurt another soul. I was determined to "make up for my sin" by helping all those who were in distress. I felt that I must somehow pay for this needless death. Because I did not have the opportunity to grieve the boy's death when I was young, I stuffed my feelings inside and acted totally unaffected. I created experiences in my life in which I could chase the pain in other people, fixing them to relieve my own guilt-tormented soul.

Here is another example of motivational factors that originate from childhood pain that lead many helpers to the nursing profession: guilt, loss of control, need to be needed, and an urgent drive to recreate and chase these painful, unresolved childhood issues. Twenty years later, I chose to pursue a nursing career in the shock/trauma unit of a large hospital, where my patients often were young adults who had encountered critical tragedies.

I was the best nurse that I could be. I took the most difficult and seemingly hopeless cases. I was driven to save the lives of countless young patients. I attached myself to their grieving families, feeling the remorse that I was denied to feel when I was fourteen. I worked endlessly, taking on double shifts, sacrificing breaks so that I could provide comfort for the patient who might die and assure that I would be there at that moment of death, never running away from my responsibility for his or her comfort. In an attempt to relieve my ancient guilt, I supported patient and family until I could no longer support myself.

About four years into recovery, I began to discover a very subtle yet shocking truth about myself: I was more comfortable — more at home — with tragedy, illness, and death than I was with joy, health, and life.

Why was I recreating this pain in my life? Why did I choose to work in ICUs and ERs? Why could I not find freedom from guilt? When would I be done with my need for high drama? I prayed for an answer, and it came in a profound and tragic way. A man with whom I had been in a relationship committed suicide in the same violent way that the boy had twenty-four years earlier. I now was given the opportunity to feel the pain, grieve the loss, and receive support from professionals and friends, not only for this recent tragedy but also for the tragedy of the teenage boy whose death I had been chasing in countless emergency critical care units.

Fourteen years of a career based on pain and guilt surfaced for healing. Each tear I shed was dedicated to one of the many traumas that I had witnessed: the pain of growing up in an alcoholic family, the pain of watching an unnecessary teenage suicide, the pain of a failed marriage, the pain of the teenager who died from what had begun as a happy ski weekend, the pain of the young mother who ruptured a blood vessel in her brain while delivering her baby daughter, the pain of the three-car rollover on Interstate 15, the pain of the many nurses who care for the pain of the many.

With the grieving came a release from the bondage of shame, guilt, control, anger, and fear. Months later as I stepped out of the shower, a feeling of completion came to me. I felt light and whole. I felt the force that had driven me for twenty years leave and a new energy enter. The exiting character in my life's theater was the darkness of tragic death. The entering character was the compassionate supporter of life. As I dried my body, I looked at the healthy glow in the mirror, and my reflection spoke to me, "You can be comfortable with joy! You can know happiness! You no longer have to chase tragedies."

Nothing is needed in our lives more than healing, both for the patient and for the healer. Codependency results from ungrieved losses. Healing from codependency demands grieving the old losses. We return to the wounds — either consciously or unconsciously — seeking to resolve our grief. If we go to the wounds unconsciously, we are like the puppy who chases his tail round and round until he finally catches it and then doesn't know what to do with it. He yelps and drops his tail when he feels the pain of his own chase, not wanting to continue to feel the pain. If we go to our wounds consciously, willing to catch and feel the pain, trusting the healing process, the chase can end in resolution.

If, however, the wounds are not treated, they may

temporarily seem to disappear, but they will reappear, especially in stressful situations. The next chapter discusses one condition that can occur when a person is exposed to intense stress and is not allowed to process, grieve, and resolve the wound. This condition is known as post-traumatic stress disorder, or PTSD.

CHAPTER FOUR

BURNOUT VS. P T S D: STRESS OR TRAUMA?

STRESS AND CODEPENDENCY: BURNOUT IN NURSING

Codependents are prime candidates for burnout. Because they have been programmed to give more than they have to give, they often give until they feel used up and empty. Because the codependent nurse is frequently an overachiever, she may take on added responsibility to relieve inner anxieties of not being good enough. For codependents, the burnout pattern repeats itself: burnout, time off, burnout, time off, burnout...

Causes of Burnout

The causes of burnout in nursing include intense, difficult, and constant helping interaction with people, as with patients who have little of their own energy and therefore drain their helpers. The more difficult a nurse's caseload, the faster the burnout occurs. Extreme caring and an overidentification with the patient is a direct factor in burnout. Monotony resulting from doing the same tasks day after day, lack of recognition, competition among peers, and noisy working conditions all contribute to burnout. Other causes include feelings of loss of control, inadequate training, and inability to participate in work decisions.

Symptoms of Burnout

The burned-out nurse may show a loss of concern or feelings for her patients. She may distance herself from her peers, arriving at work late and leaving early. She may exhibit a negative attitude towards peers, doctors, and patients, with hostile comments such as "That patient deserves what he gets." She may use dehumanizing labels when referring to her patients, calling the obese patient a whale or the alcoholic patient a sloppy drunk.

The burned-out nurse may isolate herself, become irritable, and show up to work depressed. She may have feelings of worthlessness, despair, and pessimism, which she may attempt to escape through substances such as food or alcohol, nicotine, caffeine, or other drugs (including prescription drugs). She complains of exhaustion, insomnia, and increased physical illness. Psychosomatic symptoms such as stomach upset, headaches, ulcers, skin disorders, and asthma are common.

Treatment of Burnout

With early intervention, burnout is treatable. A counselor or employee assistance personnel worker is valuable in helping the helper learn to determine the need for time off or a change of scenery. Vacations or an assignment to a different specialty can be helpful in combating burnout. Exercise, relaxation, and nutrition are essential in treatment of burnout as well as in preventing further cases of burnout.

The nurse who feels that unrealistic expectations are being placed on her by her supervisor may need to be given an opportunity to express her feelings in a meeting with a mediator who can provide her with safety to do so. The employee herself may have actually set the unrealistic aspirations, as is often the case with codependent nurses. This nurse will need to learn how to be gentle with herself. The burned-out nurse must learn to separate her work from her personal life, leaving professional stresses at work and personal stresses at home. Using affirmations such as "My care of the patients today was appropriate and valuable. I now release the patients to the next shift" are helpful. If the nurse is bored with her job, she might want to attend inservices in another specialty or apply for a new position. She might look for ways in which her patient can give energy back to her or set a goal to learn something new.

POST-TRAUMATIC STRESS DISORDER (PTSD) IN NURSING

"She is burned out. Transfer her duties from the intensive care unit to the medical floor." "Give this nurse a month off...she is suffering from burnout." When a nurse seems irritable, when the quality of her care is slipping, when her work is suffering and she rages or cries at the slightest problem — are these signs of burnout, or are they possibly signals of something more serious?

Definition of PTSD

A syndrome exists that is more prevalent in the health care industry than one would think. It is the same syndrome that many Vietnam veterans have suffered from. It has carried such names as shell shock, war neurosis, and delayed stress reaction. It was categorized under the heading of mental illness in the DSM III in 1980 as post-traumatic stress disorder (PTSD), acute, chronic, and/or delayed.

Almost one million individuals in the U.S. armed forces were involved in active combat during the Vietnam War. Through work done with veterans, PTSD has been well studied and documented. Veterans with PTSD manifested chronic lifestyle dysfunctions, including depression, sleep disturbance, feelings of worthlessness, rage, alienation, guilt, anxiety reactions, intrusive thoughts, alcoholism, and chemical dependency.

PTSD is now being diagnosed in previously untreated rape victims, adults with histories of abusive childhoods, and survivors of disasters. Kritsberg (1986) describes the syndrome of chronic shock, or PTSD, among children of alcoholics. PTSD is also being diagnosed in people who have had repeated exposure to death and trauma and increased responsibility without an opportunity to process the resultant intense stress. How can we be sure that nurses in hospice, oncology, AIDS units, ICUs, and emergency rooms or flight nurses who fly to the scenes of trauma are showing signs of burnout or are actually suffering from this syndrome, which requires a different therapeutic intervention?

Post-traumatic stress disorder has been described as a normal reaction to an abnormal situation. Say that we are driving down the freeway and see an awful accident. We admittingly tend to turn around and look, exclaim, "How terrible!", and feel the tragedy or the repulsion of the scene. In other words, we allow ourselves to psychologically process what we've seen. Say, however, that we are driving down the freeway and see not only one accident but a series of collisions. This time we may move into survival mode, gripping the steering wheel tighter, looking straight ahead, and avoiding being personally affected by the terror of the mass crisis. We freeze our feelings and push on. If not processed, these frozen feelings will eventually return, in the form of flashbacks, nightmares, startle responses, and free-floating anxiety, which can influence our work, our relationships, and our health.

Causes of PTSD

The most common experiences that result in post-traumatic stress disorder include a threat to one's life or to one's loved ones; sudden destruction of one's home, community, or property; and witnessing another person who has been seriously injured or killed as the result of an accident or violence. These traumas can be experienced alone or in a group. Both external disasters (such as floods and earthquakes, major car accidents, and airplane crashes) and internal disasters (such as bomb threats and contamination leaks) can result in PTSD.

Symptoms of PTSD

Post-traumatic stress disorder rarely appears immediately after the traumatic event: the symptoms emerge several months or even years later. People suffering from PTSD are haunted by episodes of suddenly reexperiencing the traumatic event. The memory can be a flashback so vivid that the individual feels that she or he is actually experiencing the event. The memory can come in the form of nightmares that are so frightening that the person may develop insomnia to avoid them. At times, the memories return as painful emotions and feelings of loss of control.

Another symptom of PTSD is what is known as the avoidance phenomenon. The person will avoid emotional contact with peers, family, and friends. Feelings are often difficult to identify or express, and the emotional numbness that ensues may resemble coldness, preoccupation, or boredom. Avoidance of situations that are reminders of the trauma can take place so as not to reexperience the unpleasant feelings or memories. Avoidance of responsibility may manifest because the person may be harboring fear of failure to protect those in her or his care. For nurses, these characteristics of avoidance can result in poor work records, trouble with authorities, and poor relationships with others (APA, 1988:3).

Persons suffering from PTSD can suddenly become irritable or explosive and are often described as walking time bombs. They may have an exaggerated startle reaction (hypervigilance). The slightest sound or movement can send a person into a panic attack, during which the throat tightens, breathing becomes difficult, heart rate increases, and dizziness and nausea might ensue.

Because there was no safe place to process feelings during the initial traumatic event or series of events, depression may result. As long as the individual cannot come to terms with the feelings related to the stress, the depression may control her or his life. When painful feelings come up, they are viewed as unacceptable, and people often self-medicate their pain with alcohol or other substances to dull the feelings and temporarily forget the trauma. This is especially common for nurses, who frequently have easy access to drugs.

Many nurses suffering from PTSD feel guilty because they think they did not do enough during a trauma or disaster. A nurse who was working at the time of the 1989 earthquake in Northern California commented, "I can't accept the fact that I did the best I could. I was scared, and that is not acceptable to me. I should have been able to perform better."

Personal Stories of PTSD

On Tuesday, October 17, 1989, at 5:04 pm, Northern California experienced a major earthquake measuring 7.1 on the Richter scale. In Santa Cruz County alone, all electrical power was lost, most water systems were severely damaged, and more than 600 homes were destroyed, with 11,279 additional homes receiving damage. Three acute care hospitals were within ten miles of the epicenter. Six persons in the county were killed in the earthquake, 104 were admitted to hospitals, and 1,441 were treated in the emergency departments of the three hospitals (Ward, Eck, & Sanguino, 1990:49A). Nurses who worked during this time were subject to enough extreme stress to result in bringing about PTSD.

Cumulative PTSD: Marion's Story

The more stressors a person has previously had in his or her life, the more severely PTSD will affect that person. Charles Whitfield (1989) explains that the PTSD is more serious and difficult to treat if the traumas occurred over an extended period of time, if the traumas were human in origin, and if the affected person was compelled or forced to deny the trauma or stress.

For an individual who has had traumas throughout

life, a trauma of the magnitude of the 1989 earthquake may suddenly precipitate a complex picture of delayed stress reaction. This is cumulative PTSD, built upon former experiences of severe stress.

Marion's first child died of cancer at one year of age. Spending great amounts of time in the hospital with her ill son, Marion observed the role of the nurse in the care of her child. The nurses seemed to exhibit the only sense of humanity in the medical organization. They gave Marion a feeling of warmth. When her son died, Marion decided to become a nurse.

Before she began nursing school, Marion was diagnosed with Hodgkin's disease. She again experienced the stress and impersonalization of the hospital. She developed a major hemorrhage, received 47 units of blood over four hours, and was not expected to live: "I was taken to the operating room. I could no longer see, but I could hear. A nurse took my hand, told me her name, and said that she would be there. I think of her often."

When her other children began school, Marion went to nursing college. Because of her experience with her son's death, she began working at a hospice unit in home health, where she worked for four years: "I saw some terrible things that I wouldn't admit were terrible. I stuffed my feelings about them and went on."

After several months of intensive work with patients who were all dying, Marion began to develop symptoms of burnout. When she came home from work and her children needed her attention, Marion would explode. She was empty. She needed to be needed, yet she was exhausted. People would tell her that she was wonderful. She placed expectations on herself that she should always be wonderful.

Marion began to work in a hospital as a staff nurse. She became active on many committees: "I was appalled by the injustice done to the nurses by the administration, and I felt I had to do something about it. I became the nurse representative for the union, and we went on strike. I became the enemy of administration. It was very stressful."

Each stress built upon the former stress, from the death of her son, her own life-threatening disease, hospice nursing, the committees, and the strike work.

It wasn't until the earthquake that it hit. I was at a meeting on the first floor of the hospital. We thought a bomb had exploded. The lights went off, and we were in darkness. I wanted to run. There was a lull, and the generator lights came on. We got outside, and there was a tremendous quiet. Then the sirens went off, and chaos erupted.

We organized the triaging [lining up patients for care according to the severity of their injury] outside on a grassy knoll. We worked out there until 10:00 that night. Everyone was in shock. We had prepared for internal disasters, and we had prepared for external disasters, but now we had them both. I was seeing people who were injured and imagined that everyone, including my family, was either hurt or dead. I had tremendous guilt about being there, helping everyone else instead of my family.

We had no communication with the outside world. The ham radio said the Bay Bridge was down, cars were in the water, and fire boats were trying to rescue people. My extended family lives in San Francisco, and I thought that my mother was dead. I knew our lives would never be the same. I did not know where my husband and children were until after 8:00 that night.

The helicopters came — army copters, Life Flight copters, landing and hovering over us. We thought they were going to collide! Some doctors who had been medics in Vietnam said it was the closest thing to a war zone that they had seen.

We sent critical patients inside the hospital, not knowing if it was safe. We treated all others outside: people with head injuries, cuts and compressions, fractures, chest pain, heart attacks. We were offering the repeated assurance, "Sit down, and you will be okay." I must have told a million people that they were okay! The mantra was: "I'm okay, you're okay, we're all okay, okay?" It was a bandaid statement. It was not time to ask, "What are you feeling?"

It was dark when I finally went home. Everything that could fall, be torn off the walls, or break, did. The plumbing came up through the floors. We slept in the cars. There were aftershocks all night. My only thought was, "I can't do this. I want to go away."

I couldn't go into a building for four days. Then I got a phone call from the hospital. They asked me to work, but I wasn't sure that I could ever go back. They wanted me to come to a counseling session. I said that I would drive to the hospital, but I would not guarantee that I could come in. The director of nurses met me at the door. We went inside. The nurses were telling their stories. I said the worst thing was that I couldn't be as brave as everyone else. I felt guilty that I wasn't like them.

I was scheduled to work the next day and had my first anxiety attack. I walked toward the hospital, unable to breathe, feeling my heart beating frantically. I couldn't take an elevator. I was sweaty and nauseated, and I couldn't think. I wanted to run. I held onto the staircase banister and took one step at a time. When I got to my nurses' station, I said, "I am scared and I don't know if I can do this." The nurses all turned around and said, "We're scared too!" So I stayed; they needed me.

Marion continues to feel anxiety every time she works.

Recently there was a 4.7 earthquake while I was working in the hospital. The building shook, and I became paralyzed. I wasn't sure I could walk out of the building if I had to. I have startle responses at the smallest movement. I check buildings for exit doors. I can't hear about chances of another earthquake. I am prepared in my house, but I am not prepared in my emotions.

Marion is now facing the many losses of her life.

I have lost my faith in tomorrow. Tomorrow is a calculated risk which I take each day. I am tired of traumas. I had stuffed my pain and kept going. Suddenly it all came tumbling down. All of my unresolved memories are up front. It is earth-shattering, just like the earthquake. The psychological scars are not flexible. I can't be tough anymore. I am scared. I will not be Nancy Nurse anymore.

Substance Addiction and PTSD: Carrie's Story

Individuals often turn to alcohol or other drugs to self-medicate symptoms of PTSD. Addiction to substances as well as the delayed stress reaction requires treatment. For someone who comes from an alcoholic family, the chances of addiction are great because there is a genetic predisposition for addiction and because the person learned as a child that substances numb pain.

Both Carrie and her husband came from alcoholic families. Their marriage had started to fail a year before the earthquake. Carrie's husband's drug-addicted son had come to live with them, and Carrie's mother-in-law was dying of cancer. Carrie's husband had become sexually and emotionally abusive, and Carrie was insecure and needy, full of self-hate and feelings of guilt.

At work, Carrie would sob secretly between caring for patients: "I was a wreck. Yet I was a perfect nurse, stuffing it and booming through. I helped all of the patients while I was dying inside. I began to drink a lot." Carrie's marriage ended, and Carrie purchased her own home. She had to sell her horse and her dog. She was tired. She had closed escrow on her home two weeks before the earthquake.

On October 17, Carrie was in charge of the emergency room when the earthquake hit:

> I don't know where I got the strength to do what I did that night. I wanted to crawl into a hole, but I found control. I knew we had to get the patients out of there. One of the sheriffs came in with three injured people in his car. The look on

his face was that of sheer terror. He had been downtown, and he said, "It's horrible out there." Patients were pouring in. I had to make decisions quickly. I set up the triage rooms. I designated the core part of the emergency room for gravely injured or acutely sick people. I set up the outpatient departments for minor injuries.

There were many nurses, EMTs, paramedics, and doctors who weren't oriented to the emergency room. They needed direction. We saw 175 patients between 5 pm and midnight. Obstetrics doctors were sewing up lacerations. We had a cardiac arrest in the first fifteen minutes, and many respiratory and cardiac emergencies followed. It was mass confusion.

The interim nurse manager of the department came in three hours into the disaster, wearing a starched white uniform. She paused, looked around, and asked, "Have you gotten out the disaster manual and read it?" I couldn't believe it! I had been running this disaster unit for three hours. I had it set up, and she wasn't going to tell me what to do. People wanted it to be normal. It wasn't normal.

Carrie cannot recall her feelings:

I had to be in charge. I didn't have time for feelings. I was telling everybody that it was going to be okay. Every time there was an aftershock, I would go around making sure everyone was okay. It was the way I told myself it was okay.

About four hours later, I was able to leave. When I got home, my house was destroyed.

Everything was ripped apart. The porch was off, the cabinets in the kitchen were on the floor, the back door was torn off. The toilet was lifted up and thrown against the bathtub, the hot water heater thrown through the wall.

I still didn't have feelings. I had to buckle up my emotions and go back to work. The patients kept coming. I stayed at my house until 3 am, then went to my sister's house. My sister asked if I wanted a glass of wine, and I said, 'Hell no, break out the brandy!' I had to numb in a big way. I slugged down three shots for an immediate feeling of numbness. I had so much adrenaline running that I had to keep moving. I slept for two hours on the floor, then went back to work.

Carrie could work because she was still shut down. She was pumping up on her own adrenaline. There were 77 aftershocks of 3.0 or greater during the following week. "It was like I was sleepwalking. I was dissociated from my feelings, watching from the distance as I cried."

Carrie had two days off, then she had to go back to work. She panicked:

I was sweating and hyperventilating, and my heart rate was fast. I was in a post-trauma state, but I didn't share this with anybody. I forced myself to work. I pushed myself beyond my limit. I was frightened to make decisions, but I did. I shoved everything down.

A few days later, the hospital staff had a debriefing, which wasn't helpful to Carrie, because she had already been traumatized.

Strangers were doing the debriefing. People were coming in who had no clue about what we had been through. As we went around the room, I said, "My name is Carrie, I was in charge, and it was horrible." I did not share anything else with this group, whom I didn't trust.

Carrie remembers her isolation.

Getting my home back became my major focus. My house was all I had left. I began to drink a lot to prevent feeling. I didn't have time for the pain. I had been drinking, and I called a friend who was in recovery. She told me that I needed to go to an AA meeting. So I went. That saved my life.

A year after the earthquake, Carrie became acutely ill.

I lost weight, and I was always tired. One night I went to work with a headache. Two hours later, I had severe abdominal pain. My temperature was 104 degrees. They admitted me to the hospital. I was diagnosed with viral meningitis, but they never knew for sure what was wrong. I was sick for thirteen weeks. I could barely walk. I weighed 94 pounds.

Carrie was forced to embrace her recovery. She acknowledged a higher power. She went into therapy. She opened up to her feelings. She learned that she wasn't a horrible person for being afraid. She is now working the steps of recovery and is letting go of the traumas. Still, feelings of hopelessness continue to surface:

Recently I tried to enlist in the army because I thought I could make a difference there. But the real thought was that someone would shoot me, and I wouldn't have to go on living. The bottom line was that I didn't want to live anymore.

Carrie is grateful for her recovery.

When I stop going to meetings or talking to my sponsor, hopelessness sneaks back. Now I am going to meetings and therapy and talking with my friends, and I can work again. Recovery has given me tools and support for living. It helps me out of despondency. I feel most nurses should look at some type of recovery program. I don't believe that you can be a nurse and not have the need for a 12-step program.

Anger, Avoidance, and PTSD: Anne's Story

The avoidance phenomenon in PTSD can be seen as a wall of anger that prevents family, colleagues, and friends from getting close. Feelings of estrangement from others are compensated for with outbursts of anger. As a child, Anne had witnessed displays of anger between her alcoholic parents. It wasn't until she was forty years old that Anne realized that her family had a problem with anger, even though she had been unhappy and had smoked marijuana daily for years. Her brothers also were alcoholics. After the earthquake, Anne's anger, coupled with her codependency, escalated. One year after the earthquake, because of her unresolved anger, things became unmanageable for Anne.

Anne recalls the day of the earthquake:

They were having a charge nurse meeting, so there were only three of us in the unit with ten patients. I was thrown against the nurses' station, hitting my head. Monitors were falling on the floor, and I couldn't move. We thought we were going to die. It felt like a bombing. Light fixtures were hanging with exposed wires, TVs were falling, just missing patients. It was amazing that nobody was killed. A patient's sister had been standing by the window at the end of the hallway, and the bedscale and blanket warmer crashed through the window.

The patients were in shock, yet nobody was screaming. We were all in shock ... all you can do at a time like that is keep the lid on it, because if you don't, you blow. I got up from my fall, dazed. I walked over to the window, and helicopters were landing in the parking lot. It looked like a war zone.

Feelings of betrayal and abandonment are a source of anger for Anne:

It took a long time for people to come upstairs to see if we were alive. Then they wanted us to stay up there. I told them that we would not stay in this building. It could go up in smoke any minute! I felt ignored, isolated, and forgotten. We were up on the fourth floor for hours, then when we got down, I had to stay and work. They let the other two nurses go home because they had kids, but I had to stay. I had to work an extra shift the next night. I called and told them that I didn't think I could, and they said I had no choice. I never got to stay home and process.

Anne stuffed as much fear inside of her as she could. She was smoking marijuana every day, even mornings before she went to work, for anesthesia.

The debriefing sessions came too late for Anne, who had been required to work straight through the trauma: "They had a meeting over the weekend, where a psychologist came in. He led a discussion group that was supposed to help everybody. By this time, I was mad — they were trying to fix us!"

Anne has lost much of her compassion and is now struggling to continue to work:

> I can't do this much longer. My boss knows. She asked me how I felt about nursing, and I told her that I hated it and I didn't want to do it much longer. My relationships have suffered. I am paranoid and distrustful. I am impatient and intolerant. I want control. I have flare-ups at each anniversary that last for months.
>
> I have been a nurse for ten years. This is it for me! I am trying to find a way to get out of nursing. I hate it. I have no psychosocial skills anymore. I don't want to hear my patients' problems. I don't go to staff meetings or work extra shifts, and they {authority figures} don't like that. If my patients are dependent and grabby, trying to suck me dry, I punch out their call light. I tell them to make a list, and I will take care of everything at once. I don't see anything wrong with that. Nurses look at me like I am cold, and I reply, "Who do these patients think they are? They have to get with it." I hate to think that I am not

compassionate, but I am not going to make myself sick! I am at that point now, I am done.

Anne is in individual therapy for PTSD.

The issues I am dealing with started with the earthquake and now are getting deeper. I am finally understanding how sick I really am. I have PTSD from my birth! This PTSD just uncovered my other PTSD. I can't stuff it anymore. I am trying to understand boundaries right now. I have this big territory around me I've been trying to protect.

Anne tries to reassure herself that it will never happen to her again:

I carry my car keys in my pocket. I have told my supervisors that the next time anything like that happens, I am leaving. I am walking out of here, going home, and they can deal with firing me. They will see when the time comes. I am not risking my life for these people. I don't owe them. I paid my dues. If they want to stay and die, they can. I won't.

Job-Related PTSD: Julie's Story

Post-traumatic stress disorder is not limited to traumas such as earthquakes and wars. Nurses who have worked in critical areas such as shock/trauma intensive care units and emergency rooms can experience symptoms of PTSD and have no idea why they are having so much difficulty in their lives. Julie was such a nurse. She might have stopped the tragic implications of

PTSD had she paid early attention to the signs of burnout. Instead, she continued to expose herself to a work area where a great many of her patients died. She pushed through the initial burnout, judging herself for not being able to take it like the other nurses.

Julie survived by stuffing her feelings. As patients lay comatose around her, she joined in cynical jokes about their conditions. When a patient died, she did quick post-mortem care, cleaned the bed, and prepared herself for the next tragedy. She used marijuana to numb out each evening, refusing to process her feelings because she did not know where to go that would provide the safety for her hidden vulnerability. Her pain became her greatest secret, even to herself.

After two years of working with tragic cases, including gunshot wounds, suicide attempts, car accidents, and surgical disasters, Julie began to experience nightmares. She recalls one such dream:

> I walked into my bedroom and became angry because my patients had all followed me home and were now lying there bleeding in my bed. I could even smell the decay of dying people in my dream state. I tried to get the patients out of my bed, but as I grabbed one by the arm it fell off, and I started to scream.

Julie increasingly isolated herself, avoiding her friends who were not connected with the hospital. She became irritable, and her job evaluation mentioned her outbursts of anger. She began to use amphetamines to keep going and to bring her a sense of control over feelings of panic. She experienced difficulty sleeping and had frequent bouts with illness.

By the time Julie entered therapy, she was addicted to multiple substances, had alienated herself from friends and family, and judged herself as a failure at work. Julie has found her recovery from PTSD frightening and difficult. She is required to emotionally return to the patients who haunt her, recall the terror of tragedy and death, feel the grief and anger, and heal the wounds of her profession.

Treatment of PTSD

PTSD can be successfully treated using a variety of methods, including individual, family, and group therapy. Mental health professionals can help people work through the trauma, resolving grief, anger, and fear.

Individual Therapy

Individual psychotherapy focuses on examining personal values as well as on how the traumatic event violated those values. The goal of individual therapy is to promote self-esteem and self-control. It is important when choosing a therapist to find one who is working through his or hier own issues of codependency.

Family Therapy

Family therapy may be necessary when the behavior of the person suffering from PTSD affects other family members. Family therapy focuses on communication skills, effective parenting, and stress management techniques. The goal of family therapy is to open up communication by encouraging the PTSD survivor to feel and to talk about his or her feelings.

Group Therapy

Group therapy is an effective treatment for many

people suffering from PTSD. Survivors are encouraged to share with others their experiences of the trauma and their reactions to it. Group therapy provides support as well as a reality check for group members, who help each other to realize that the trauma was not their fault. This allows survivors to release their feelings of guilt and unworthiness.

Issues addressed in both group and individual therapy include problems with relationships, feelings of betrayal, victimization, career changes, and chronic illness. Help is given with identifying feelings, backbiting behaviors, isolation, and chemical dependency (including alcoholism). Clients are guided through the stages of the grieving process, including denial, anger, bargaining, and acceptance.

Support Groups

Twelve-step groups and other programs of self-awareness are often a beneficial adjunct to group and individual therapy. Nurses who work such programs seem to cope with trauma and stress more effectively than those who do not. They learn to process and deal with stresses at the time they occur and not stuff them. One of the first things people in twelve-step programs learn is to "Let Go and Let God."

Debriefing

The initial goal of debriefing was to reduce the number of psychological casualties among service personnel after traumatic events or a critical incident. Debriefing provides crisis intervention through support group discussion with trained mental health professionals. It allows ventilation of emotions and serves to keep communication open between workers. It helps the individual to deal with denial, hostility, anxiety, feelings of helplessness and guilt, withdrawal, fear, and depression. It is meant to help alleviate problems of sleeplessness, flashbacks, alienation, nightmares, and the avoidance phenomenon (Rubin, 1990).

The Initial Phase of debriefing consists of introducing the team, presenting the rules of confidentiality, and explaining the purpose of debriefing. The next phase is the Fact Phase, during which participants tell what their jobs were the day of the traumatic event. Everyone can see what happened from all perspectives, instead of from just their own point of view.

The Thought Phase follows. A nurse explains this phase: "The participants share the first thing they remember thinking. Often fear can be identified in explanations such as, 'My son could be dead' or 'When will the building fall down?' Most of the time people don't know what they were feeling, because they were numb through it all; but they can identify thoughts."

Further phases of the debriefing session include the Reaction Phase, where the participant describes the worst part of the incident; the Symptom Phase, where unresolved issues and stress reactions are discussed; and the Teaching Phase, where stress management techniques are presented.

Many nurses in hospitals suffer from PTSD. They are the walking wounded. Since nurses traditionally numb their feelings anyway, they are likely to be severely affected by trauma. Weekly and monthly debriefing sessions are beneficial. Nurses must know that it is okay to have feelings.

A before-shift assessment in a stressful nursing unit would give the manager a tool to help the staff provide safe care to the patients. The manager might ask the staff in the morning, "On a one-to-ten scale, where are you today emotionally?" If one nurse is at a two level and another is at an eight, the critical patients might be assigned to the emotionally stronger nurse. If a nurse begins the day at a nine and decompensates to a two, the manager may assess what has changed. This is a nonjudgemental system, which gives the nurse permission to be valued as a person and not feel she has to be a perfect nurse.

An after-shift debriefing would enable the nurse to process, then leave behind, the stresses of the day. This is not the same as "change-of-shift report." This is for the helper, not for the patient. It might sound like this: "I am so tired of taking care of patients with diarrhea! If I have to change one more bed..." or "Mrs. _____ is so close to dying. It is really bringing up my own fears of my mother dying. When I look at her, I see my mother. I feel guilty for not telling my mother I love her enough." Listening is the only skill that is necessary in this debriefing. The environment must be safe, confidential, nonjudgemental, supportive, and loving. It is especially helpful to have a facilitator who does not work with the patients.

RECOVERY IN ACTION: GORDON'S STORY

Gordon is a Vietnam combat veteran. He was a firefighter for five years and a paramedic for three years before he started nursing. He was driven to help people in crisis. It seemed he couldn't get enough. He found himself becoming a workaholic:

At age 38, I had hypertension, I had an ulcer, and I carried nitroglycerine in my pocket. I finally got out of emergency room nursing because of the stress and worked in a chemical dependency unit. I found I related with the patients and later discovered why: I am now in recovery for chemical dependency.

Gordon was drafted at 19 years of age. He was exposed to medicine while being treated for a hernia in a Vietnam army hospital. "I wound up in a mash unit, where I had an operation. The nurse gave me special care. After spending five months in the army hospital, I got into nursing. I started as an emergency room aide."

Gordon did not think he had symptoms of PTSD at the time he started nursing, even though he was smoking marijuana daily. But after being in veterans rap groups for three and a half years, he found that he had been covering up his anger with drugs.

I was frustrated that I never got to take it {the war} out on anybody. I had been in an ambush, people died from stepping on boobie traps, but we never saw the people who were shooting at us. I never got even. I was left with a feeling of incompleteness. Now I know that this was a normal response to an abnormal event.

At the time of the 1989 earthquake, Gordon was in charge of the emergency department where he worked.

When the shaking started, I looked around to see if everybody was okay. A patient with an IV was under his bed, an EMT was draped across another patient. The nurse I was working with and I crawled under the counters. The shaking finally stopped, and I said, "We have to get ready."

I stayed until 3 am. We had over 100 patients that evening — in an eight-bed unit. One of the first was a woman whose crushed leg was hanging by tissue. The police brought her in in the back of their car. All ambulances were busy. The wound was filthy, and the other nurse whispered, "I can't do this." I said, "You know what to do. Get an IV in this woman. Get someone here to take care of the leg. Just go do that."

We had no clue how bad it was. We thought San Francisco was the epicenter, then we heard that downtown Santa Cruz had been destroyed. We heard that a tidal wave was coming. We didn't know whether to go up to the second floor — which was unsafe from the earthquake — to escape the tidal wave. We found out later that it was a rumor. Rumors were flying.

A surgeon came for the woman's leg, and he looked at her and said, "I can't do this!" I had to take his arm, walk him over, and say, "We need you to do this. The surgery team is waiting for you. The generator is working. What will you do first?" He shook and said, "I'll change my clothes." He did it.

People started showing up in panic, and I would put my arm around them and say, "It's okay. We will help you get back out there where you need to go. Have a seat over here." I was calm. I had a sense of everything being okay, that a higher power was directing the show, and I surrendered my will.

Having been in recovery for over three years before the earthquake, Gordon had learned to feel his emotions. "I did not numb my feelings. I checked in with my feelings regularly. I would stop, move to a corner, and ask myself what I was feeling. I didn't block it. I was open to the experience, and whatever happened I was ready to accept it. It worked!"

Not only has Gordon worked with his veterans group, but he also attends twelve-step meetings. His recovery program is based on a strong relationship with a higher power and a sense of divine law. He is able to stay in the moment, trusting that God is in charge. "I believe that traumatic events like earthquakes happen to tell people that their way isn't working. They dissolve the ego's will. They get people in touch with another power higher than themselves."

As a result of surrendering to a higher power, Gordon does not today experience delayed stress. Because of his work in recovery, he is awake and in touch with his feelings. "I see a difference between a nurse who is not in recovery and the recovering nurse who has a sense of a higher power. Because nurses not in recovery have no tools, they do it their way. Even though they may not use medicines (some of them do), they block the crisis and feelings out in whatever way they can. They cannot be there for their patients. They have barriers up. I see many frightened nurses who were working during the earthquake. They have no hope, because they don't have any tools. They are using all of their vacation time, their sick time. They drag their feet and do the bare minimum. There is no closeness. Sometimes I want to fix it, but I realize that I can't."

Gordon has learned how to care for himself first. "When I feel out of balance, I either go to a meeting or go to an acupuncturist and drain those negative energies. I feel what is going on. I don't have to medicate. When I feel crazy, I stop and ask myself what is going on."

Gordon expresses his belief in recovery: "It seems that when two nurses come from dysfunctional homes, the one who is in a recovery program can take life's experiences and use them as assets, where the other nurse can take the crisis as the last straw or use it as an adrenaline fix and pump it through."

PREVENTION OF BURNOUT AND PTSD

Here are some suggestions for preventing burnout and PTSD:

Lower your expectations.
Take a break between tasks.
Take time to read books on how to reduce stress. If you don't have time to learn about ways to reduce stress, you need to take the time. It means your time is being taken up doing too much — which leads to stress.
Tune in to your feelings on a regular basis.
Find a safe place to talk about your feelings.
Learn to say no. Then say no.
Say yes to yourself.
Put yourself at the top of your list of priorities.
Learn that you are not the only person who can do it.
Learn to be a human being, not a human doing.
Learn to ask for help.
Be gentle with yourself.
Laugh.
Practice doing one thing at a time.
Listen.

Breathe.
Stretch.
Close your eyes.
Clench your fists and then relax them.
Reacquaint yourself with your heart.
Reacquaint yourself with your higher power.

CONCLUSION

Nurses need tools to treat burnout and PTSD. Right now, most nurses are going it alone, waiting for someone to give them the tools. The situation is serious. It goes beyond acuity, it goes beyond DRGs, and it goes beyond cutting staff and budgets. The nursing profession has a propensity for a cunning, baffling, and powerful disease, whether it be manifested in chemical dependency, codependency, or PTSD. If nurses continue to do things on their own — which is what they were taught — the time will come when their way won't work any longer. It will cost too many nurses their health, and the cost is too great.

Carl Jung wrote that the concealing of one's emotions "is like psychic poison which ... cuts off the unfortunate possessor from communion with his feelings." People need to feel safe to process their experiences and emotions. They do not need to be judged — either by themselves or by their peers — for feeling vulnerable. PTSD and burnout can be treated — even prevented. The remedy comes in the awareness of the causes and the symptoms and in the treatment of these two conditions. Table I compares burnout and PTSD.

TABLE 1

BURNOUT VS. P T S D

BURNOUT	PTSD

CAUSES

BURNOUT	PTSD
Constant and intense interaction with people you are trying to help.	A psychologically distressing event or series of events.
Too many contacts — overload.	Fear, terror, or feelings of helplessness.
High level of difficult patients.	A threat to one's integrity or life.
Monotony — no variety in job.	Sudden destruction of home or community.
Lack of recognition.	Seeing a person(s) who has been seriously injured or killed as result of an accident or violence.
Competition.	Natural disasters (earthquakes, floods).
Crowded, noisy working conditions.	Accidental disasters (car or airplane).
Lack of control.	Deliberate disasters (bombings).
Lack of training for burnout.	Repeated exposure to trauma.
High ideals and expectations.	Child abuse.
Meaningless work.	Sudden loss of loved ones.
Overidentification with patients.	
No participation in decisions.	

SYMPTOMS

Loss of concern for patients.	Survival guilt.
Distancing from peers (isolation).	Repeated memories with painful emotions.
Negative attitudes toward people.	Flashbacks — strong reexperiencing of the event(s).
Dehumanization of patients.	Distressing dreams of the event(s).
Loss of temper. Anger and envy.	Distress at events that resemble the trauma.
Feelings of hopelessness, trapped feelings.	Avoidance of stimuli associated with the trauma. Avoidance of feelings, thoughts, activities, or situations.
Easily rejected.	Inability to recall the trauma (psychogenic amnesia).
Pessimistic about work and life.	Diminished interest in activities.
Increased reliance on crutches (alcohol, other drugs, including nicotine and caffeine, and food).	Feelings of estrangement from others.
Chronic exhaustion.	Inability to have loving feelings.
Sleep disturbances.	Sense of foreshortened future (no hope for tomorrow).
Susceptible to colds, flus.	Sleep disturbances.
Overreaction to annoyances.	Irritability, angry outbursts.
Easily distracted.	Difficulty concentrating.
Psychosomatic symptoms (ulcers, stomach upset, headaches, dermatitis).	Hypervigilance, startle responses.

Suicidal thoughts.

Physiologic reactivity with exposure to memories (sweat, tremors).

TREATMENT

Talking about it.

Individual psychotherapy.

Exercise, nutrition.

Family therapy.

Relaxation (naps, meditation).

Rap groups, peer counseling.

Lower level of aspiration: accept limitations.

Medication (when appropriate only!).

Vacations.

Physical care and nurturing (acupuncture, nutrition).

Vary work patterns.

Biofeedback, stress management.

Separate work from rest of life.

May require inpatient intensive treatment.

Improve working conditions.

Resocialization classes.

Twelve-step programs.

Twelve-step programs.

*Source: Jane Zahn, Ph. D., of Santa Cruz, California.

For many, writing is an important part of recovery from delayed stress. The following poem by Mary Tyrell, RN (1987), portrays her personal experience as a nurse in Vietnam.

HINDSIGHT

"Why write about it now?"
My thirteen-year-old asks.
What difference does it make?
What bearing on her life?
Reared in this home
With a Dad who visits weekends.
I wonder
If her parents had met in Duluth, instead of Guam.
Taking a break in Naval uniforms,
the idyllic Pacific creating a mood
On this island eight miles wide.
The wounded men and B-52s,
Military maneuvers, geographical bachelors,
A need to be close.
The nurses' quarters hummed with distractions:
News from home
Twiggy fashions;
China for hope chests;
Glen Campbell in stereo;
Thursday night happy hour.
Some nurses cracked and disappeared
from humid tropical weather,
80-bed wards, sans air conditioning.
The wounds, the waste, the loss.
I reread those letters sent home.
No mention there of war and pain,
Casualties and stress.
I need to write it now.

Nurses work in one of the most stressful professions there is. Exposure to tragedy, suffering, and death is unavoidable. Nurses are there to help, but they cannot help if they are suffering themselves. The next chapter discusses one manifestation of burnout and PTSD: chemical dependency.

CHAPTER FIVE

CHEMICAL DEPENDENCY: A FATAL SYMPTOM

VICKI'S STORY: PART ONE

Vicki is a registered nurse who grew up in an alcoholic home, where she learned at an early age how to take care of others. During her nursing career, she frequently drank after work, being careful that her drinking patterns would not resemble those of an alcoholic. She assured herself that she was always in control. While working at a hospital, she remembers one time seeing a wine commercial on the TV in a patient's room and starting to salivate, which upset her. She found, however, that if she focused on the patient in another room who was spitting up blood from an alcoholic liver, her drinking, by comparison, didn't seem to be a problem.

Another time, an elderly patient refused to take the Tylenol with codeine that Vicki had prepared for her. Vicki knew how codeine felt; she had once been given a prescription for it. Instead of discarding it, she put it in her pocket, thinking, "This is ok, because otherwise it would have been wasted." Vicki thought that she could use it for her own sore back or tired muscles after a hard day at work. This seemingly innocent moving of the pill from her patient's medicine cup to her own pocket soon became a move from her pocket to her mouth, a movement that would repeat as often as possible.

When her first child was born, Vicki established a relationship with pain pills. The dependency progressed quickly, and by the time Vicki returned to work, her addiction was as important a reason to be in the hospital as her need to help others. The pills interrupted her terrible feelings of guilt about her unhappiness with her husband, her family, and her career and about her inability to fix her alcoholic father. She was driven instead to fix her patients. The more guilt she felt, the more pills she took, causing more guilt and increasing the need for her regimen of self-medication.

During the next three years, Vicki found more opportunities to take drugs from the hospital. She had accepted a job as assistant head nurse of her unit. Vicki developed a ritual of arriving at work early to inspect the medication assignments before her shift began, identify the patients who had narcotics prescribed, and assign herself the patients who required the most drugs. An efficient and studied nurse, she knew the dosages well. She played doctor, nurse, and pharmacist, all for herself. She had complete control over how she felt.

When Vicki again became pregnant, she was devastated. How could she continue to take her narcotics? Since Vicki's former nursing instructor had had a retarded child because of drug usage during pregnancy, Vicki was aware of the probability of her own child's being affected. Vicki recalls, "When I realized I was pregnant, I remember thinking *not*, 'How am I going to quit these drugs so that this baby will be healthy?' but rather, 'How messed up is this baby going to be because of my drugs?' I did not even consider quitting as an option."

By now Vicki suspected that her drug usage was out of control. She found herself apologizing to her unborn child while she was taking the drugs, knowing that it was no longer her choice. When the baby was born, Vicki received anesthesia, but by then her tolerance to drugs was so high that the pain medication did not seem to alleviate her discomfort:

> After the baby was born, I had surgery to tie my tubes, and I could feel everything. I was screaming. I knew I was going to die of pain. They hurried through the procedure, not understanding why it hurt me so badly. The anesthesiologist gave me nitrous oxide, but that was not enough. I couldn't tell them that I had been taking so many drugs that these feeble attempts meant nothing. When the procedure was over, they gave me a shot of Demerol. Suddenly everything was wonderful. I was euphoric, full of love and nurturing. Demerol took me where I wanted to be. It was ordered for me for a couple of days. One night, as I was getting a shot, something inside of me clicked. I knew that I had developed a lasting affair with Demerol.

When Vicki returned to work, she was once again full of feelings of guilt. Her baby had been born with a heart murmur from the drugs, yet Vicki could tell no one. One night at work, Vicki decided to shoot up Demerol. During the following year, she progressed to IV usage of over 700 mg. of Demerol in one shift (an average dose of

Demerol is 25 to 75 mg IM). As assistant head nurse, she appeared to be functioning fine. Occasionally someone would comment that she looked tired, but nobody suspected her drug thievery or abuse. Vicki would chart that she had wasted the drugs and then would give them to herself. Her illness progressed to the point where she began to substitute phenergan (a medication for nausea) or saline for the patient's drug, administer the substitution to the patient, and take the drug herself.

Once Vicki ordered twenty vials of Demerol from the pharmacy and kept ten of them for herself. She would do anything to get her drug. On evening shift, when the patients were still drowsy from their surgery, she would take their drugs herself, as it was hard in this groggy state for these patients to determine whether they actually received their medication. Vicki's disease spread like wildfire, yet none of her peers or supervisors said anything.

One night Vicki walked into a confused patient's room and found the patient's gown was off and his IV tubing disconnected. While she was looking for the other nurses to help her clean up the mess, another patient asked her for help. Irritated, Vicki leaned into the room and screamed at him, "Just a damn minute !" Vicki had never before spoken to a patient like this, but this time she was entering into withdrawal and needed more drugs in her system to cope with taking care of everyone else. Still nobody said a word.

Once, before leaving work, Vicki self-injected so much medication that she fell asleep at the wheel of her car, driving it over the curb into a tree. Her car destroyed, her mind questioned, "Why didn't I die?" She then realized that her drug usage was out of control. But the disease of addiction is cunning, baffling, and powerful.

Vicki moved into denial, rationalizing that she had been such a perfect nurse, working until she was exhausted, then hitting a tree instead of running into someone's house. Vicki kept using drugs, and the problem continued to escalate.

Three months later, Vicki received a phone call from her head nurse following a weekend off. The head nurse asked Vicki if anything had looked suspicious on Friday when she counted the narcotics: they suspected some tampering. Vicki's first thought was not of remorse, but of sheer panic: what would she do for her drug source? She had enough drugs for only a few more days. She denied any knowledge of the nursing unit's drug problem.

By Wednesday, Vicki was out of her drugs. Feeling extreme guilt, she contemplated suicide. What was wrong with her? Why couldn't she shake this thing? Was she that weak? Suddenly she realized that she was already committing a slow suicide with her drug addiction. She knew that she must get help. Vicki called her sister, who thought that exhaustion was the problem. After all, Vicki served on many committees, giving much of herself in service, her children were young and demanding, and she had a stressful job. This was the role Vicki had always played in her family: the helper, the saint, the martyr.

Vicki finally told her husband that she had been taking drugs from the hospital and giving them to herself for three years and that she was hopelessly addicted. The color drained out of his face; he had not suspected, even though he had noticed bruises on her thighs where she had been shooting up. In his denial, he had silently been convincing himself that she had cancer or leukemia.

THE PROBLEM

Chemical dependency is a reality in any health care institution. It lurks around the corners of the ICU, the surgery suite, the emergency room, and the nursing home. It hangs on the key rings for the narcotics drawer, tempting, seducing, and promising the nurse a sure way to help her push harder, to serve more, and to feel less. Leading researchers have estimated narcotics addiction among nurses to be 30 to 100 times greater than it is among the general public and that the populations of the equivalent of ten nursing schools are lost to narcotic addiction each year (Jefferson & Ensor, 1982:8). This suggests that any one nurse in any one hospital may be caring for her patients while chemically impaired. Nurses bring addiction into the workplace, where there is a perpetual necessity for life or death decisions.

Millicent Buxton and Marty Jessup, of the Bay Area Taskforce for Impaired Nurses, state that alcoholism and other drug dependencies affect an estimated 220,000 nurses in the United States. Buxton and Jessup facilitate a support group for recovering chemically dependent nurses in San Francisco. Studies done among this group of recovering nurses revealed that :

> • 51 percent of nurses in the group have legal charges pending (licensure and/or criminal justice system).
> • 78 percent of nurses in the group did not use drugs prior to becoming a nurse.
> • 55 percent of the female nurses first self-administered a psychoactive drug working in critical care (ER, ICU, CCU) areas.
> • 75 percent of the male nurses first self-

administered in critical care areas.

• 65 percent of the group reported that another family member also had alcoholism or another addictive disease (personal citation, Marty Jessup, 1992).

At the Haight Ashbury Clinic in San Francisco, Millicent Buxton and David Smith conducted some of the first research on chemical dependency in the nursing profession. Through their admirable work, they found a significant increase in deaths among nurses related to alcohol and other drugs. According to coroners' reports in San Francisco during a forty-three-month period, there were thirty nine deaths of nurses where the primary cause of demise was alcohol or other drug related. Thirty-nine deaths in forty-three months in the San Francisco area alone (Milkman & Shaeffer, Chapter 12).

Our nurses are dying, and we are still in denial. Denial is a major aspect of all addictive diseases, according to Buxton, who believes that denial among nurses "has led to dangerous risks to patients and has perpetuated addictive disease among nurses." [*]

DENIAL

The disease of chemical dependency *cannot* exist without denial. Chemical dependency is a life-threatening disease when it is covered up. Denial is not uncommon. People do not see what is too difficult to see. A recovering nurse reflects, "I knew that my peers noticed, even though they did not confront me. Finally I was asked to resign because I wasn't learning fast enough. That is denial! Everyone knew I was using."

In a study of alcoholism in the helping professions, LeClair Bissell asked a population of recovering alcoholic nurses whether there had ever been a colleague or superior, no matter how informal the admonition, that directly addressed the issue of excessive drinking rather than a secondary problem such as lateness or poor job performance. Bissell reports, "Throughout their entire drinking careers, more than three quarters of the nurses could not remember anyone ever saying anything critical to them about their drinking" (Bissell & Haberman, 1984:72).

A nurse specialist in the chemical dependency unit of a university hospital conducts inservices for nurses. She addresses the tremendous denial among nurse supervisors as well as the staff. This denial is indicative of what is known as institutional cobehavior and functions similarly to the denial in an alcoholic household, where the unspoken rule is "Don't think, don't feel, don't talk." Nurses often go unchecked, with no intervention, until they hit bottom. The nurse specialist explains that for nurses, often the last thing to go is the job, that nurses will live out their role as perfect nurses until the end.

This nurse specialist shares her message of concern: "I worry about the average nurse who thinks that it cannot happen to her. I want everyone to know that chemical dependency doesn't have much to do with what you do or how perfect a nurse you are but has to do with how you feel inside and what you are doing with chemicals."

Margo worked in a shock/trauma intensive care unit, where the physical and emotional demands were frequently overwhelming. She recalls working a night shift, caring for two patients in critical condition, when she became very ill, passing a kidney stone. The pain was excruciating, and Margo called the night supervisor, who firmly stated that Margo must stay, as there were no nursing replacements available.

The supervisor handed Margo two Tylenol with codeine, advising her to "take them and carry on." Margo finished her shift chemically impaired, with the support of her supervisor and the little white pills, and "carried on" to an addiction that nearly killed her. This nurse supervisor clearly carried the message of denial for the sake of being a perfect nurse giving perfect patient care.

PROFILE: THE IMPAIRED NURSE

There is no typical impaired nurse. When we attempt to define a pattern, we limit ourselves in our search for those who need help. We do know that chemicals change baseline behavior, often causing increased irritability with patients and colleagues. Frequently the impaired nurse is socially isolated from her peers and avoids breaks and lunchtime conversation. She may become moody and argumentative during her shift.

An impaired nurse rarely misses work, partially because the workplace is her source of drugs, but also because of her identity as a "good nurse" who is needed. Her life could be in shambles, but her job performance convinces her that she is okay. A nurse's self-esteem is often based on work, and the chemically dependent nurse is seen as an overachiever. An impaired nurse often receives excellent work performance evaluations, yet any suggestion for improvement can cause feelings of failure. When the disease progresses to a state of unmanageability, the chemically dependent nurse begins to make mistakes, which only confirms her already well-established feelings of shame and guilt.

The chemically dependent nurse may want to work nights only, when supervision and social demands are at a minimum. She may have a strong interest in counting the narcotics and volunteers to be the medication nurse. Her isolation appears to be dedication as she busies herself with tasks rather than socializing during quiet times.

Her use of alcohol and other drugs is not intended for a recreational high, but rather is self-administered medication for pain, fatigue, or depression. She does not use street drugs as much as she uses prescription drugs obtained through physicians or stolen from her patients. She is not typically an intravenous user, although if her disease progresses to the use of needles, she may wear long sleeves to prevent detection of track marks on her arms.

She knows her drugs well, their effects, their dosages, their half-lives, their adverse reactions. Her addiction becomes a science of careful titration of drugs for desired outcome which will enable her to take care of her patients more effectively.

The impaired nurse may not have a history of alcohol and other drug abuse. In fact, because 83 percent or more of chemically dependent nurses come from families where alcoholism and/or other drug abuse was present (Schaef, 1987:30), nurses often are adamant that, as Claudia Black expressed it, "It will never happen to me!" In a support group of twenty-five chemically dependent nurses, 100 percent said that they had come from families where alcoholism was present.

The nurse who has a propensity for addiction just

requires the right (or fateful) chain of circumstances — fatigue, overwork, accessibility to narcotics, and external focus of care — to become captive to chemical dependency in a comparatively short period of time.

Alcohol remains the number one drug of choice for the nurse as well as for the general population. Demerol remains the second drug of choice. Nurses who want to numb their pain use Demerol, morphine, and alcohol. Nurses who thrive on the high drama of the critical care unit often have an affinity for cocaine and amphetamines.

ROBERT'S STORY

Robert, a male nurse, was apprehended following an investigation of the theft of Demerol from a thoracic intensive care unit at a large university hospital. Robert's story stirs feelings of sympathy not only for the nurse but also for his patients, supervisors, and the hospital as a whole. Robert had previously worked in an emergency room in another state, where he had been caught stealing drugs and was asked to leave. He was a hard - working man, the father of five, staunchly religious, often seen at baseball games with his sons. He carried a great deal of responsibility as a father, a church member, and a critical care nurse.

Robert's pattern was to take a package containing ten vials of Demerol from the narcotics drawer and slip it into his pocket, then go quietly to the bathroom, and slit the plastic package open with a razor blade. He would extract the Demerol from the ten vials in the package with an empty syringe and refill the vials with saline or, when he didn't have saline with him, unsterile tap water. He would then seal the contaminated vials back into the original package and replace the package in the narcotics cabinet. The drug substitutes were then unknowingly administered by the nurses on duty, often intravenously, to patients after open heart surgery.

One night Robert was found asleep in the corner of the ICU after he had overmedicated himself. He was finally suspected for diverting drugs and required to give a urine sample to substantiate the evidence. It was not until Robert was arrested that he asked for help. This was his bottom, his crisis, his golden opportunity for growth. Had he not been caught, he might have died from drug addiction.

CAUSES OF ADDICTION: OCCUPATIONAL FACTORS

Accessibility to Drugs

One factor in the predilection for drug addiction in nursing is a high level of accessibility to drugs. Nurses are exposed to a pharmaceutical candy store with many types, flavors, and desired effects. Every time a nurse opens the narcotics drawer, she is subject to temptation. If this availability is combined with other factors such as fatigue, pain, denial, and perfectionism, it is easy to understand the motives of the impaired nurse.

Fatigue

Difficult shifts and fatigue from unusual sleep patterns add to the enticement that drugs may have for the nurse. Many nurses have families at home to care for, demanding energy from an already diminished source. The nurse may consider drugs to aid her in overcoming exhaustion.

Pharmacologic Optimism

Another reason that nurses have such a high propensity for substance addiction is the "general pharmacologic optimism that reflects trust and reliance on chemicals for their therapeutic value" (Buxton & Jessup, 1984:131). Nurses see the relief that the medication gives their patients who are in pain, and they grow to trust and anticipate the outcome. When a nurse's own back hurts or when a headache may be interfering with her giving quality nursing care, the nurse may be tempted to try a little codeine to help her through her shift.

Nurses in the ICU daily observe the miracle of drugs, waking their patients up, putting them to sleep, taking away pain, wiping out defenses. Since the nurse has developed a naive sense of control when she sees that she has the power to reverse anything she puts into her body with the appropriate antidotal drug, she uses less caution in administering higher dosages.

Spiritual Pain

An emotionally wounded nurse who cannot comprehend a sense of divine order may view substances as a way to numb the pain and anger directed towards God and the injustice of suffering and needless death.

FAMILY HISTORY, ANOTHER CAUSE: CAROL'S STORY

Carol's father was an alcoholic, and Carol remembers when her father would come home drunk in the middle of the night and beat her mother and her sisters. Carol would beg her father in vain to stop abusing her mother.

Her mother divorced him, but not before the emotional wounds had been inflicted.

Carol married an alcoholic at age nineteen. Her husband and his friends drank cases of beer every day, which Carol viewed as normal. Before Carol became an RN, she frequently drank alcohol and used cocaine, which gave her feelings of superiority. After she received her nursing license, she replaced her drinking with pills, which she used intensely for the next seven years:

> I didn't start out by taking pills from the hospital. I began by going to see doctors for my back pain, and for stress. I had a lot of dental work done, and the dentist gave me Percodan. The doctors would give me anything I wanted because I was a nurse, and I knew what I needed, right? But what I needed was more, so I started stealing from the hospital.

When she finally decided to quit cocaine, Carol was getting prescriptions for pain pills, which she later began to take from the narcotics drawer and from her patients. Carol would sign the drugs out, saying that she had given them to patients, and put them in her pocket. Often she would give plain Tylenol and would take the codeine herself. She felt guilty and frightened, but Carol had no choice. Carol's most important goal for the day was to implement her plan to get her medication. She had convinced herself that she could keep helping other people as long as she had her supply and could anesthetize herself.

For years Carol would return home to a drunk husband. She was chronically depressed, and the pills made her feel better. When her marriage finally ended,

Carol moved so that she could "clean up her act". Three months later, Carol's husband followed her, and they attempted a reconciliation. Soon after, Carol again took pills from the hospital where she was working. Within four weeks she was caught. Carol recalls this time with emotion:

I was working night shift. I was having trouble sleeping in the day, so I started signing out the drugs and giving them to myself. They checked some patients' urine for drugs. The tests were negative after the patients were supposed to have been medicated. The director of nurses and my supervisor told me that I was not allowed to work anymore. They said that an investigation had been made, and that I couldn't return to work until it had been cleared up. I asked them what it was about, even though I knew. They said it was about some Tylenol #3 (codeine) that was missing, and they would not tell me any more.

I was sent to the sheriff. I felt like my world had fallen from under me. I became hysterical. I was angry at them for catching me. How dare they do this ! ! How dare they suspect me! They told me that they were going to put me in jail. The sheriff asked me what had happened to the drugs, and I denied everything. I said that I gave my patients what I charted. Then they told me about the urine specimens and how much trouble I was in, that they could throw me in jail and charge me with a felony.

I started to cry and a policeman said, "Now will you be honest with us?" A man was sitting across the room and quietly said that I needed help. He could assist me in applying to a recovery program for nurses through the California Board of Registered Nursing, called The Diversion Program. I could enter the program, and the charge would be a misdemeanor until I finished the program. Then it would be removed from my record.

The suggestion for the diversion program came from the sheriff's office and not from the hospital. I found no support at the hospital. They said, "Send her to jail, turn her over to the law." I went back to the hospital and talked to my supervisor, who told me that he would see about taking me back after my recovery program was complete. He said roughly, "Go home and get your life together," as if I were a criminal. I found no support at the hospital, from any of the doctors or nurses or the administration. The pharmacist was out to get me.

Carol entered a treatment center for a month, during which time she learned that a common pattern of addiction is the desire to escape, to numb the pain. She learned that she had not been able to cope with life on life's terms. She discovered that she had been externally focused on helping others. She had not learned to take care of herself. Carol is currently in a two-to-five-year diversion program and has returned to work.

Once Carol had been accepted into the program, she entered a residential treatment program and then was required to consistently attend Alcoholics Anonymous and Narcotics Anonymous meetings. She met with a panel of RNs and a psychiatrist from the Board of Registered Nursing, who determined her treatment program. She also met regularly with OHS (Occupational

Health Services).

It took a lot of courage for Carol to go back to work at the hospital. Many people didn't want Carol there. The doctors exclaimed that they would not trust her again, that if they ordered Tylenol with codeine, they would not know whether the drug went into Carol's pocket or to the patient. People talked about Carol, but Carol was able to cope by trusting that it would take time to repair her image.

> Every day that I walk into the hospital I remember the day I was sent to the sheriff's office, when my life fell before me. That memory will never go away. Opening the narcotics drawer ' now, I think, "Is the pharmacist watching me?" I know that I am being watched, even after a year and a half.

Narcotics are still disappearing at Carol's hospital. Carol recalls her first day back on the medical/surgical unit. Carol had been given the keys at about 7:00 am, and by 8:30 there were six Vicodans missing from the narcotics cabinet. Carol heard people talking and felt that all eyes were on her. But she remembered what she had learned in treatment: if questioned, volunteer for a urine test, which she did. When her test came back negative, she told those who suspected her, "You obviously have another problem here, and you'd better start looking somewhere else."

When speaking of the Diversion Program, Carol states that it is a mixed blessing. Although it saved her nursing career, it is no easy or quick fix:

> The Diversion Program wrote up a strict

contract, which I have to follow. Every six months, I meet with someone from the program who assesses how I am doing. I am required to go to four AA meetings a week, and I give a urine specimen randomly. I am also required to take fifteen units of continuing education every two years on chemical dependency. This will continue until the committee feels I am ready to complete the program at which time my record will be clean.

I feel that we need a nurse support group in this small rural town. There is so much denial. We really do need help for the helper. We nurses require a mixture of AA, Al-Anon, and ACOA meetings. Add to that our career, which only encourages codependent behavior, and we are sitting ducks!

NURSING DIVERSION PROGRAMS

The Nursing Practice Act (NPA) defines The Diversion Program as "a system designed to identify and seek means to rehabilitate registered nurses whose competency may be impaired due to use of drugs or alcohol or due to mental illness." The services this program provides include confidential consultation, intervention, assessment and referral for treatment, development of a rehabilitation plan, monitoring for compliance, and support (pamphlet, "Registered Nurses In Recovery," BRN California). The diversion program is described as an avenue that "provides hope, help, and alternatives for registered nurses experiencing alcohol, chemical dependency and emotional problems" (pamphlet, "Registered Nurses in Recovery," BRN California).

Since its inception in October 1985, the California Board of Registered Nursing's Diversion Program has evaluated and referred over 1,000 registered nurses. Of these, approximately one-third have successfully completed the two to five-year program, one-third are still actively participating in the program, and one-third have left the program or have been terminated for noncompliance. In fiscal year 1990/91, the California Board of Registered Nursing revoked the licenses of seventeen registered nurses for substance abuse. Seventy-six percent of all the registered nurses on probation with the Board of Registered Nursing were disciplined as a result of chemical dependency (Jill Thomson-Skeoch, Diversion Program Manager, Jan. 30, 1992 .)

As of January 1992, only thirteen states in America had passed legislation to initiate diversion programs. If there are an estimated 220,000 nurses in the United States who are chemically dependent, these programs are clearly not reaching a vast number of nurses with a potential for either a recovered life or a tragic death.

The Diversion Program is difficult and does not pull any punches about the seriousness of a nurse's actions. The program in California is stern as well as compassionate, requiring that the nurse take full responsibility for her recovery over an extended time period. It acts as an advocate not only for the nurse but also for the consumer. The California Diversion Program lists as its objectives:

1. To ensure the public health and safety through a program that provides close monitoring of nurses who are impaired due to chemical dependency or mental illness.

2. To decrease the time between the nurse's

acknowledgment of a problem with chemical dependency or mental illness and the time he or she enters a recovery program. Early entry into a recovery program will allow the nurse to practice nursing in a manner which will not endanger public health and safety, is more cost-effective than traditional discipline programs and is more cost-effective for the nurse.

3.   To provide a program for affected registered nurses to be rehabilitated in a therapeutic, nonpunitive and confidential environment.

4.   To provide an alternative to the lengthy traditional disciplinary process.

5.   To reach nurses who may be affected by chemical dependency or mental illness who are not being reached through the current disciplinary system.

6.   To provide a program that can refer nurses to services that are within their economic means (California Board of Registered Nursing Diversion Program description, revised 9/87).

Criteria for admission to The California Diversion Program are strict. The registered nurse must be a resident of and be licensed in the state of California. She must agree to undergo medical and/or psychiatric examinations for evaluation of appropriateness for the program. The nurse must cooperate by providing medical information, disclosing authorizations, and releasing liability as requested. She must agree to cooperate and must not have had a previous discipline for substance abuse or mental illness, or have been terminated from a diversion program (California BRN Diversion Program, 9/87).

RECOVERY:
VICKI'S STORY, PART TWO

Vicki, the nurse described at the beginning of this chapter, explains the beginning of her recovery:

> One day I was in the basement, where our pharmacy is located, and an assistant head nurse was there with the narcotics clipboard. They had found the narcotics inventory sheet where she had ordered the twenty vials of Demerol. I walked up to her and I whispered, "I'm your Demerol thief." She put down the board, gave me a hug, and said, "You're going to be okay."
>
> We walked up to the head nurse's office, and I told her everything. She leaned over to me and asked, "Are you an ACOA?" I had read everything I could on addiction because I had wanted to do a study on it to fix myself. But adult children of alcoholics issues were something I did not want to touch. The head nurse told my that I needed to go into a treatment center and take a medical leave. Suddenly I had a feeling of relief inside me.
>
> My supervisors have been very supportive of me. My former head nurse came to see me often. She told me that she still loved me and that I was sick, not bad.

Vicki entered a treatment center for a month for chemical dependency. She was told that she would not be alive much longer if she didn't address her addictions.

When she was admitted into a detoxification bed, the woman in the next bed was withdrawing from cocaine. Vicki cringed as they put the ID band on her wrist.

Vicki could hear the nurses talking at the nurses' station and found herself identifying with them instead of with the patients. Identifying with the helper instead of the fellow addict is one of the largest problems for a nurse entering recovery from addiction. All day long Vicki would listen to the talk at the nurses' station, fantasizing that she would soon become a chemical dependency nurse.

Vicki had helped others for so long that she believed that requesting aid for herself was a sign of weakness. It was overwhelming for her to acknowledge the part of her that needed help instead of always being there to serve everyone else. She was so detached from her feelings that she often was not even aware that she needed help. She also struggled with low self-esteem and feelings of guilt about stealing drugs for her own use.

Vicki had to overcome her subservient and resentful attitude about doctors. The doctor on staff was there to help her, and she had to learn to accept his help. She and the doctor soon developed a healing relationship, and the doctor introduced Vicki to the wounded child within her. When Vicki first met her little girl self, she was surprised to learn that she had not been a happy, bouncing little kid, nor had she been a self-confident youth. She had been, and still was, a hurt, scared, and traumatized child.

Being the perfect student and nurse, Vicki felt that if she studied hard enough, she could do a crash course in recovery. A tough realization was that it wasn't going to be a quick fix. Vicki was so used to fixing things, including herself, that she thought she could do this recovery and be done with it. She was to learn about the difference between healing and fixing.

When Vicki left the treatment center, she received a six-month medical leave from work. At the end of this time, she felt ready to return to her job, but her support group talked her into staying out for one more year. The nurses in the group explained to her the dangers that they saw. It was difficult, yet Vicki knew they were telling the truth. She knew she had to learn to love herself before returning to work, or she would again fall into being there for everyone else and neglecting her own needs.

After a year and a half, Vicki went back to work. Her unit had moved to a new building, a move she speaks of as symbolic of her own transition:

> We now look across the court at our old building. At night, I can look into the room where I used to throw up. It is really powerful, because they are now tearing that old building down.

Vicki's support group dealt with the issue of the transition of going back to work, ACOA issues, and other issues specific to nurses. Vicki recalls the facilitator of her support group once declaring, *"I do not want to do the disease of nursing anymore! "* Returning to work has been a positive experience for Vicki. The leader of the nurse support group had advocated that nurses in recovery return to work when they feel they are ready to go back with dignity, carry the narcotics drawer keys when possible, and reenter the job as a whole nurse. She believes that if a nurse decides to leave her job, it should be because she wants to and not because she is forced to.

Fortunately, Vicki was prepared for opening the narcotics drawer by her nurse support group:

There is a sign imprinted on the inside of my eyelids with a little skull and crossbones on it, saying, "Instant Death." At times the drugs still talk to me. Today my neck was tight from a lot of stress. One patient's discharge orders included a large bottle of Percodan. I thought, "He wouldn't miss 10 cc's." It was a subtle, seductive thought, and it almost knocked me over. But I recalled another nurse from the support group, also addicted to Demerol, who recently relapsed after returning to work and was taken to jail. Her legal problems will follow her everywhere.

One day all the little packages, bright and colorful, were talking to me. I don't think there is a drug in there that I haven't taken. I remembered the effects, thinking, "Oh yeah. Dilaudid didn't last very long, but it felt great. Morphine made me nauseated, so I have to mix it with something for nausea." This day, each drug became animated. The drugs were tempting me. Then I got a clear message from my God/Self that they all lead to death. This is what I have to address now: do I really want to be in a seductive setting? A recovering alcoholic is not going to choose bartending as his career. If this drawer continues to talk to me, I will leave. I care enough about myself now to not want to be in a dangerous environment.

Vicki has a message to the many nurses who still suffer, who are not yet able to acknowledge their own illness in the midst of caring for others:

I know that if I stay sober, I will carry the

message of hope to other nurses. My dependency wasn't all my fault. The system around me fosters dependency. A nurse is to carry on, no matter what, denying her own problems and her own needs. The nurse who initially discovered the Demerol missing used to be my enemy. Her honesty and refusal to be in denial were threatening to me. Now I quietly thank her for facilitating my recovery.

RECOVERY ISSUES

Control and Perfectionism

When treatment is initiated, perhaps the most difficult issue a nurse must face is letting go of control and accepting the role of the patient who needs help. We have helped others for so long, and our identity is one of the survivor, the saint, the sunshine in the midst of the storm. How can we be comfortable with the tears of surrender when we have been wiping these tears from the faces of our patients for so long?

Nurses tend to be perfect students and seem to have a need for straight A's in recovery. It is difficult to let go of the need to be good. I think back to when I was admitted to a treatment center. I was determined to do everything perfectly. I studied all of the books, reading the entire Big Book of Alcoholics Anonymous in a few days and starting to work on the twelve steps of recovery as if I were going to take a final exam on them.

Not only did I hand in all my assignments early, but I helped the other "patients" with theirs, making myself available for everyone else instead of surrendering to my own concealed pain. I was a nurse, through and through.

I was known as Susie Sunshine because I was the one the patients came to when they needed cheering up. I knew how to help the others, but I had no concept of my own needs.

When I was ready to graduate from the program, I went to an evaluation meeting to hear my prognosis for staying clean and sober. I was sure that I had been the shining student who would receive praise for helping the other patients. Imagine my shock when I received my prognosis: "Guarded!" Terror surged through my body as I tried to comprehend the words. The counselors told me that I had been so externally focused, so busy helping others, that I had not surrendered to accepting help for myself.

Tears streamed down my face as I continued to struggle for control. But this time, no control was to be found. I had been found out, and I no longer had the title of registered nurse to hide behind. I was powerless, and I had no answers. I went to the chapel and fell on my knees, surrendering for the first time to a power greater than my small ego self. I uttered the unacceptable words, "Help me," and with those two words, I felt the loving arms of my counselor around me. "It's okay," she whispered. "You do not have to be a nurse right now. It's okay."

This release of control is an essential step in the recovery process for nurses. A residential treatment center provides a safe place to let go and let God and allow others to serve the server. Studies (Robbins, 1987:17) show that 90 percent of impaired health care professionals who go through an in-patient center have a successful recovery and that 85 percent who seek treatment can return to the workforce as productive employees. It is far more cost-effective for an employer to encourage an impaired nurse to seek recovery than to risk the cost of a lawsuit that may result from a nurse working under the influence of narcotics and to fire the nurse only to have to incur the expense of training a new nurse.

Guilt

The nurse may feel extreme guilt about having stolen drugs from patients and about having possibly caused harm to those whom she was driven to help. When finally given the privilege of carrying the keys again, the nurse will require support for feelings of paranoia and fear that everyone is going to suspect her if drugs are missing. The paranoia is not without justification. It may take time for peers to trust again.

Returning to Work

Other issues specific to the nurse's recovery center around returning to work. The nurse may be subject to legal action if she has been charged with diverting drugs from her patients or the hospital. She may also be subject to a strict contract with the diversion program, resulting in feelings of guilt if she cannot carry her share of the load because she is not allowed to carry the narcotic keys, be in charge, or work nights or overtime. The nurse can feel shame about her peers knowing that she stole drugs and have feelings of low self-worth, believing that she is no better than the drug abusers who wind up in hospital emergency rooms.

Family of Origin

Other recovery issues originate from a dysfunctional family of origin, such as alcoholism, incest, or codependency. Support groups such as Al-Anon, Adult Children of Alcoholics, Narcotics Anonymous,

Codependents Anonymous, and Emotions Anonymous are valuable. The nurse's high expectations of self are relieved as she accepts the concept of disease rather than weakness.

Support for Dealing with Issues

Recovery issues are addressed in nurse support groups as well in a regular structure of AA, NA, and other appropriate self-help groups. In the program of Alcoholics Anonymous, the nurse receives the message of commonality, as she is among people other than nurses here. She learns that she is a person who happens to be employed as a nurse, not a nurse who happens to be a person. She develops friendships with people from many walks of life. The program of AA has proven effective because of the principle of one recovering person helping another. The helper does not need to have a license to help, and the licensed helper learns to receive help from others like her.

INTERVENTION

Techniques for proper intervention published in many professional journals and books for nurse managers who are faced with the sensitive issue of a chemically impaired nurse include nonjudgemental and early intervention based on job performance and personal concern, confidentiality, referrals to available services, and documentation of all incidents and events relative to the situation. A helpful resource, available through the American Nurses Association, is a pamphlet entitled "Addictions and Psychological Dysfunctions in Nursing: The Profession's Response to the Problem."

POLICIES AND PROCEDURES

Published guidelines should be available in a policy for the recovering nurse who is returning to work, for the protection not only of the consumer but also of the institution and the nurse. A contract between the institution and the nurse is recommended that should regularly be evaluated by the nurse, the supervisor, and a chemical dependency treatment provider.

Guidelines for the treatment of chemical dependency in the nursing profession are well studied and documented. The Board of Registered Nursing in each state would be an appropriate place to obtain more information.[*] The purpose of this book is to state the gravity of the problem and to share the hope for a solution.

PREVENTION THROUGH EDUCATION

When speaking to students in nursing schools, I ask how many of them come from alcoholic homes. Frequently the majority of students raise their hands. Information must be presented to these students at an early stage of education. Educational facilities have a responsibility to teach risk factors and initiate the self-awareness process before chemical dependency and codependency surface in students' future careers.

Nursing schools may find it helpful to require students to attend Al-Anon and Codependents Anonymous meetings as well as AA, opening up the discussion to explore why they have chosen this field and how they can enter the profession with an awareness of the risk factors.

Hospital inservice departments may offer continuing education to working nurses through staff meetings, sponsored seminars, and nursing lectures. Education on the subject of chemical dependency must be provided by state nurses' associations. Continuing education units should be offered as a motivational incentive for nurses to learn of the risk factors, prevention, and peer intervention.

THE IMPAIRED PHYSICIAN

Chemical dependency is not limited to nurses. The American Medical Association estimates that one in ten physicians is impaired by alcohol or other drugs (Jefferson & Ensor, 1982:8). Buxton and Jessup claim, "Denial of the disease in the physician is the primary obstacle for recovery. The stigma of addiction, combined with professional roles, personal expectations, as well as their role as the healer, prevents early intervention and treatment" (1985:30). Physicians and nurses are the two professionals who are most likely to develop addiction to hard narcotics such as Demerol and morphine (Bissell & Haberman, 1984:72).

I recall my orientation when I was a new nurse. I was thrilled by the opportunity to observe open heart surgery. I dressed in the scrub uniform, pushed my hair under the little paper hat, then made my way to the observation point designated by the surgeon. Eagerly, I stood on a stool near the anesthesiologist.

I don't remember much about the case, as my attention was drawn to the activities of the anesthesiologist, who was mixing up two syringes of

Valium for every one that the patient received. Not only did I witness him preparing the syringes, but I watched as he shot the extra syringe through his pant leg. Shortly after this, he excused himself, put the patient on automatic settings, and went to the doctors' lounge. A few minutes later, he reappeared, laughing loosely, speech slurred. As he settled back to monitor the patient, he started to nod, and he soon fell asleep.

I was upset, and I sought out my supervisor for advice on whom to report this to. The supervisor took me into her office and flatly told me, "You do not report this to anyone. You may not have seen what you thought you saw. This doctor is one of our best, and I advise you not to make waves." At the time, and for a long time after that, I believed her observation that I may not have seen what I thought I saw. But my vision was validated years later when I walked into a meeting of Narcotics Anonymous and heard this same doctor telling his personal story of drug addiction. He had been in recovery for a year, and his story was touching as he shared the secretive ways that he used to get his drugs during surgery.

THE IMPAIRED NURSE AND IMPAIRED DOCTOR: A DEADLY COMBINATION

The combination of the chemically impaired nurse and the chemically impaired physician can be deadly. When a young doctor named David and I got together, our seemingly controlled lives quickly became uncontrolled, and the disease of addiction almost cost me my life and eventually sent David running from state to state in a sequence of hospital disasters.

I was an ICU nurse supervisor and was highly respected for my work in the management of the intensive care unit in a rural hospital. I had started new educational programs for the nursing department, was on the faculty at the local college of nursing, and taught critical care seminars and advanced life support classes throughout the state.

I was a single mother of two, which required me to constantly be available for either the hospital or my children. Coming from an alcoholic family, I was naturally driven in my dedication to helping as a symptom of the need to be needed. When I wasn't at the hospital, I carried a beeper to assure that I could be there at any time, night or day, when someone needed my help. Little did I foresee the help that *I* would soon require.

David came into town as the new anesthesiologist, and we soon became known as the perfect couple. But along with his past, David brought with him the chemicals that not only fed his own dependencies but also activated my latent addiction. Within one year, we were both caught in the cycle of overwork, drug thievery, and isolation, hopelessly lost in the incomprehensible demoralization of chemical dependency.

When David first introduced me to speed, I was hesitant, yet in a quick decision that changed my life, I tried this seductive drug. I immediately felt superior, in control, and powerful. I had found a medication that I believed could actually help me to be a better nurse and enable me to endure more, think clearer, and act faster. My underlying depression and feelings of self-doubt left me.

Because my feelings of self-worth were dependent on my image of the perfect nurse, I was unable to see the cunning powers of what quickly became my "demon lover." The seductiveness of this chemical was subtle.

My relationship with this drug, and consequently with others, was based on the false promise to make me a better helper. By the time I realized that I had been courted by this tempter, my choices had been removed. I needed my drug just as my patients needed me.

David's and my drugs of choice were cocaine and amphetamines, drugs that were financed by the large salary of David's medical practice, but our medication routine was not limited to stimulants. We would blend these drugs with doses of any substance that David had stolen from the day's surgical procedures.

When the high from the stimulants became unbearable, David would draw up dosages of tranquilizers that would enable prolonged usage of more drugs. David's house became a miniature pharmacy, stocked with drugs that had supposedly been given to his surgery patients. Vials of Valium, Demerol, morphine, and other narcotics lay on his table with syringes and bags of cocaine.

At times, David's beeper would sound, and David would rush to the hospital to help with an emergency surgery after taking a large dose of Valium. On these occasions, he would take a little cocaine so that he could perform and would then enter the surgical suite chemically impaired, shielding his trembling hands from view behind the sterile screen where he sat monitoring the patient under anesthesia.

All moral values were tossed aside for the sake of the substance. Yet I carried out the job of supervisor for the ICU in perfect control. If a patient died after a hard shift of trying desperately to save him, I would use drugs to mask my pain and anger. If a patient survived as a result of "my hard work," I would use drugs to celebrate the victory.

My staff was now talking about my nerves, worried about my health, yet totally unaware of my disease. They became sensitive to my moods, and as my weight dwindled, they tried to convince me to eat more. By doing this, they were being codependent as they continued to try to fix their head nurse.

My hands were constantly trembling, and soon I found that my first stop when I got to the hospital was the pharmacy box, where I would take a beta-blocker medication that would relieve the tremors. My next stop was the bathroom to self-administer a little amphetamine so that I could feel sharp enough to carry out the tasks as supervisor of the intensive care unit.

One day, a doctor confronted me about my health. I had a chronic sinus infection, I was constantly fatigued, and I had dark circles under my eyes. The doctor asked me if I needed help. I denied that anything was wrong, and the doctor admitted that he thought I had been hiding the disease of cancer. His denial may have been that he never even suspected drug abuse.

Complaints were being brought to the director of the hospital about David's erratic temperament in the operating room, yet no suspicion of drug abuse was ever verbalized. As David's disease progressed, his relationship with the other doctors became tense. Nobody wanted to do surgery with a man who screamed at the nurses, cussing and blaming others for *his* oversights. Nurses were becoming frightened of him as his demands increased and his patience decreased. David's technique became sloppy, breaking sterile field with sneezes and careless movements. Still nobody admitted to suspecting drug abuse as a cause for his bizarre behavior.

I was experiencing anxiety attacks, and my drug-induced paranoia was beginning to interfere with my judgement. I obsessed about saving my patients, taking personal responsibility for the life or death of those in the critical care unit. I had developed symptoms of congestive heart failure and toxic manic/depression. I needed help. I suffered in this quiet prison of addiction until I finally collapsed and began the long and painful journey of healing the healer. I worked right up to the day I was admitted into the psychiatric hospital, with nobody suspecting that this nurse was a drug addict.

Once I had entered a residential treatment center, the other physicians at work finally started to become suspicious of David. They did not know of my drug addiction; my supervisor told them I had been admitted for exhaustion. Instead of initiating a proper investigation or registering their concerns with the AMA, the physicians quietly asked David to leave. When last heard of, David had been "quietly asked to leave " three other states and had not as yet been reported to the AMA or counseled to seek help.

CONCLUSION

Nurses are needed. They are needed to help their fellow nurses who still suffer. Denial is dangerous. Turning one's head, pretending not to notice the smell of alcohol on a peer's breath or a peer's trembling hands as she tries to write progress notes on a patient's chart, serves neither the nurse nor her patient.

The next chapter discusses the healing institution itself and the possibility that it, too, might need healing.

Resources Available for the Chemically Dependent Nurse

- Addictions Nursing Network, 1631 3rd Avenue, New York, NY 10128.
- American Nurses' Association (ANA), 2424 Pershing Road, Kansas City, MO 64108, (816) 474-5720.
- California BRN Diversion Program, Diversion Program Manager (916) 324-2986, Program Contractor and 24 hour emergency 1-800-522-9198.
- International Nurses Anonymous, 1020 Sunset Drive, Lawrence, KS 66044, (913) 782-3707.
- National Association of Alcohol & Drug Abuse Counselors (NAADAC), 3717 Columbia Pike, Suite 300, Arlington, VA 22204, (703) 720-4644.
- National Consortium of Chemical Dependency Nurses (NCCDN), 975 Oak Street, Suite 675, Eugene, OR 97401 1-800-87NCCDN.
- National Council on Alcoholism (NCA), 12 West 21st Street, 7th Floor, New York, NY 10010, (212) 206-6700.
- National Nurses Society of Addictions (NNSA). 2506 Gross Point Road. Evanston, IL 60201, (312) 475-7300.
- NCADA — Bay Area, 1049 Market Street, Suite 507, San Francisco, CA 94103-1605.
- Nurses' House in New York (Manhattan), for emergency funds for nurses in need.

* Statement of the Problem, Bay Area Taskforce for Impaired Nurses.

* In California, there is not only the Board of Registered Nursing but also many other resources, such as Millicent Buxton and Marty Jessup's noteworthy organization, the Bay Area Taskforce for Impaired Nurses at the Haight Ashbury Training and Education Project in San Francisco.

CHAPTER SIX

THE ADDICTIVE SYSTEM: INSTITUTIONAL COBEHAVIOR

TERMINOLOGY

System

Webster's New Collegiate Dictionary defines a system as "a group of interacting bodies under the influence of related forces." A system contains an interrelationship of all its parts. One person coming from a system in which she or he was influenced by dysfunction will carry that dysfunction into future systems unless it is recognized and dealt with.

Addiction

Anne Wilson Schaef and Diane Fassel define addiction as "any substance or process that has taken over our lives and over which we are powerless. Addiction, say Schaef and Fassel, "begins to have control over us in such a way that we feel we must be dishonest with ourselves or others... It leads to compulsiveness in our behavior... (and) serves to numb us up so we are out of touch with what we know and what we feel" (Schaef and Fassel, 1988:57).

Addiction need not be to alcohol or any other substance. It can also be to a process. While a *substance addiction* is an addiction to a mood-altering substance that leads to increased physical dependence (Schaef, 1987:20), a *process addiction* is an addiction to "a specific series of actions or interactions" (Schaef, 1987:22). A process addiction is growth inhibiting and counterproductive and can be as fatal as any substance addiction. Among hospital personnel, process addictions can include addictions to crises (in the emergency room), to misery (in oncology or AIDS wards), to struggle (decreased personnel and increased patient load to save a failing budget), or to martyrdom (working a double shift because one's self-esteem depends on it).

The Addictive System

An addictive system is a closed system in which the members feel powerless, develop survival patterns, and function using learned addictive behaviors. An addictive system operates by the same rules as the dysfunctional family. Robert Subby (1984:26) identifies these rules: "Don't talk, don't feel, don't rock the boat, be strong, be good, be right, and be perfect." These oppressive rules exist within an addictive system. When the expectations — even the criteria for performance evaluations — include these rules, the members are working in an addictive system.

TYPES OF ADDICTION

In their book *The Addictive Organization*, Schaef and

Fassel (1988) describe four types of addiction inherent in the addictive organization. The book is a pioneering work on a subject that has long been hidden in denial. The four types of addictions can apply to a dysfunctional health care system:

1. *The key person as an addict* . Mary Riley describes key person addicts as those who... "isolate themselves from the normal feedback that other employees encounter. They surround themselves with codependent managers/staff/friends who feed their addiction. The addiction is often to control. Those who confront the addict are quickly removed. In this closed system, only positive feedback is allowed" (1990:17). An example is the director of nurses who hires codependent nurse managers who are willing to blindly follow their leader.

The key person addict may be dramatic, dogmatic, depressive, paranoid, or compulsive. His or her leadership style is dishonest and manipulative, and the key person may use gossip and rumors to manipulate. If a situation exists with an employee that threatens to expose the manager, the manager may use personality conflict as an excuse to take the focus off of his or her behavior that is being challenged. This causes a "me against them" picture. Codependent workers jump in to protect this addict manager, who gathers codependents around for protection.

2. *Codependents and addicts in the workplace* . Behaviors for this group include perfectionism, workaholism, rigid thinking, crisis orientation, difficulty with teamwork, trouble with authorities, people pleasing, and acting out. Here is a replica of the dysfunctional family helping to maintain a closed, secretive addictive system. In *Co-Dependency: An Emerging Issue*, Robert Subby (1984) stresses that codependents and addicted medical people

need treatment and that helping is a sophisticated con that protects an addiction.

3. *The organization as the addictive substance* . Like any addictive substance, the organization can present illusions that alter the moods of the workers. Ambiguous missions and goals bring a false sense of dedication to the nurse who trusts the addictive system. The nurse who sees that these missions and goals are not the priority of the hospital may experience disillusionment, followed by dysphoria. An addictive process (e.g., ideal goals and missions) makes a person feel good and creates a dedication that is not based on authentic values. It also causes an emotional hangover when the illusion is finally recognized for what it is.

4.*The organization as an addict* . The organization itself may have all of the characteristics of an individual addict, including indirect communication (such as numerous paper memos that conflict with previous memos), which is confusing. Memos are a way of avoiding direct confrontation. Another dysfunctional type of communication is the gossip chain, which excites the staff and creates control for the initiator.

Scare tactics are an example of the gossip chain used to keep the focus away from the addict. When staff members of one hospital heard that they had six months to shape up and become more productive or the hospital would close its doors, nurses were seen frantically trying to cut down patient care hours and trim their staff. Addictive organizations use crises to "excuse drastic actions on the part of managers; (crises) heighten an organization's tolerance for addictive behavior" (Woititz, 1989:160).

Other characteristics of the organization functioning as an addict include manipulation, frozen feelings (as a result of the manager who exclaims, "Get control of your emotions!"), forgetfulness of purpose, distorted thinking (including externalization, projection, and blame), and dualism (discussed in the following section).

CHARACTERISTICS OF THE ADDICTIVE SYSTEM

Anne Wilson Schaef has been an influential leader in the field of addictive systems. In her book with Diane Fassel, *The Addictive Organization*, she describes the characteristics of addiction as they apply to the system, including denial, dualism, confusion, dishonesty, perfectionism, scarcity model, control, frozen feelings, ethical deterioration, crisis orientation, depression, stress, forgetfulness, dependency, negativism, projection, tunnel vision, and fear. Some of these traits are discussed here, and to the list I add workaholism, guilt, broken promises, secrets, and competition between peers. The characteristics of addiction function to keep the addictive system alive. You may wish to reflect on them to see if your institution or staff fits the descriptions.

Workaholism and Perfectionism

Workaholism is an unrealistic self-imposed demand to do it all. It is based on the premise previously discussed as the Messiah Trap: "If I don't do it, it won't get done" (Berry, 1988:6). Perfectionism is an unrealistic self-imposed demand to always know the answers and to never make mistakes. The perfectionist or the workaholic may have filled the role in her or his childhood of the family hero whom everyone counted on to save the day. Family heroes, who hold it all together, make efficient managers. Family heroes also make excellent crisis intervention nurses, who are willing — even prefer — to take over the added responsibilities resulting from short-staffing emergencies.

Crisis Orientation

Crisis orientation provides an illusion of control and a feeling of aliveness. For the addictive system, things run "normally" during a crisis. Intensive care units function efficiently when they are geared up, waiting for the "train wreck" (a crisis in which patients arrive in critical condition) in the emergency room. The radiology department eagerly awaits the critical patient who is coming for an emergency angiogram with life support systems in full operation. Everyone feels a sense of teamwork along with an adrenaline rush, and everyone seems especially animated. At these times of crisis, there is an overall feeling from the administration of economic and job security, and the director proudly watches "her nurses" while offering to run for supplies.

Admittedly, teamwork and efficient functioning by the staff are what a good hospital is all about. They are the bonding force that makes the team strong. A good trauma team and supportive ancillary members are indispensable, and lives are saved when jobs are done well. The addictive system, however, *needs* crises for its sense of esteem, for a quick fix, for the rush of adrenaline. An addictive system will invent a crisis when there has not been one for a while. If there is no crisis, people feel nervous about who is needed, their rank, and their purpose. Management may demand more productivity, or there may be cutbacks in staff. When things go too smoothly, rumors can increase, complaints are frequently filed against peers or physicians, and staff get restless, inventing some problem to focus on. All of these invented crises produce more stress.

In an addictive organization, everyone plays from an old dysfunctional tape of guilt, control, and fear. One nurse explains her hospital's messages of crisis and scarcity to the employees: "We are now working at 111 percent efficiency (i.e. doing better than 100 percent of the expected rate of efficient performance) while being told to sign out early if we can, not work overtime, and reduce the staff. ICU is working at 125 percent efficiency and are still demanded to work harder. This is stress!"

Control

Stress is a result of a person's need to be in control. A nurse who creates or contributes to stressful situations at work may be trying to gain a sense of control in a situation that has become uncomfortably quiet for her. A manager who is demanding of her staff may be attempting to "keep us afraid, out of touch with ourselves, and too busy to challenge the system" (Schaef, 1987:13).

Myths Related to Control

Schaef (1987:46-47) describes three myths, or illusions, of the addictive system that are all related to control:

1. The addict "is innately superior." The addict is anyone who needs to control another, whether it is a staff member, a physician, or the administration, because everyone else is inferior.

2. The addictive system "knows and understands everything." The daytime administrators mysteriously know how hard the night shift works, the director of nurses understands the staff nurses' problems, and the nurses know just how severe the patients' pain is. *Anything unknown does not exist, and anything "new or*

different cannot be tolerated", and thus "must be concealed or maniulated — controlled."

3. "It is possible to be God." An ICU nurse may participate in the role of making life or death decisions from the ego rather than from a sense of moral values. Being God gives one "the ability to *control* everything."

Dualism

Dualism is a method of control that assumes that there is always a right way and a wrong way. An example of dualism is the war that rages between full-time nurses and per diem (as needed) nurses. In the staffing office it is often assumed that regularly staffed nurses are more dedicated and therefore more "right" than per diem nurses. Yet there is a need for both types of nurses, and the solution may not be an either/or position, but rather an appreciation of what each nurse can offer the institution.

Ethical Deteriorization

Schaef explains that ethical deteriorization occurs when "the addictive society creates God in its own image to suit its own purposes.... this distortion further separates us from our spirituality and our awareness of ourselves as spiritual beings" (1987:91). Medical ethics dilemmas occur frequently in ICUs, where judgement calls of whether to allow someone to die or to extend the patient's life with life support are inevitable. A nurse in the ICU of a teaching hospital expressed her frustration of taking care of chronic schizophrenics who have been deteriorating for twenty years and of performing unnecessary procedures on them for the sake of a learning experience for the residents and medical students.

Many questions of ethics in the hospital and home care settings exist, some of which frustrate the nurse who feels powerless over the physician's decisions. An example is the full code status (to do everything possible to resuscitate, including chemical and mechanical intervention) on an aging patient in the geriatric care center. One nurse stated, "I have problems with the doctor who orders a full code on a 94-year-old patient who is ready to die. Patients will beg you to let them die, and you aren't allowed to honor their wishes. This is hard to be around, eight, ten hours a day, looking at the fatigue and the fear in their eyes, the fatigue of their families." Because it is often too painful for the nurse to see her elderly patient pumped on, intubated, shocked, and catheterized, she may push down her feelings of rage and injustice.

Frozen Feelings

Frozen feelings in an addictive system refer back to two of the previously mentioned rules in the dysfunctional family: don't talk and don't feel. The nurse is frequently required to shut off and block out feelings of fear, anxiety, anger, even joy and excitement. Many nurses claim a numb, feelingless state upon the death of their patients. They explain that their feelings would become liabilities because there is no safe place for them to experience or express them.

A group at an emotional release workshop was expressing grief for the facilitator, who was dying of cancer. Everyone cried together and healed together. A nurse in the back of the room quietly admitted to the group that he could not feel: that expressing grief was foreign to him. He worked in an emergency room and witnessed death every day. He declared, "Death is a relief when you can finally stop pumping on the patient's chest. Feelings just get in the way!" While working with this man's emotional blocks, the group identified an injustice in health care professions: the necessity of helpers to freeze feelings so that they can *be there* for their patients. This is a survival issue, because grief and tragedy can become overwhelming if feelings are allowed to be felt.

One helper states, "If we become personally involved and experience feelings, we would lose our ability to help. We would become a hindrance to the healing process. In being professional we often have to be so callous and indifferent to feelings that we become like robots. I sometimes wonder if our motivation for doing this kind of work in the first place isn't related to our need to gain power over feelings of helplessness. The real tragedy is that we become so good at deluding ourselves that we lose touch with our own souls."

Denial

Unable to find a safe place to feel, the nurse who works with tragedy resorts to the defense mechanism of denial, the key protecting agent in the addictive system. When we refuse to experience and feel what we see and know, we are denying our personal reality. The challenge is to break through our denial and give the discomfort (or disease) a name (addiction). Identifying the organization as addictive — or the individual as codependent — does not condemn or judge that system or person. It opens the system or individual to healing.

Secrets

Snow and Willard describe dysfunctional families as closed systems that receive messages, many of which are secret, from the top down. They state in their book, *I'm*

Dying to Take Care of You, "Dysfunctional health care organizations operate much the same way {as dysfunctional families}. The secrets they keep often are masked by looking good, allowing only certain issues to be discussed, and keeping nurses and their concerns for organizational issues diverted to the next crisis — instead of talking straight, listening, and dealing with issues as though nurses' perceptions mattered" (1989:81). Refusing to participate in the denial is an act of love.

Projection

Projection is a form of denial. Rather than deal with feelings of anger, grief, or fear, the nurse might project these "unsafe" feelings onto patients, peers, or administrators. Projection takes place when the nurse becomes emotionally attached to her patient and has him or her live out unsafe feelings to lessen her own deep anxiety. This may be a nurse who gives too much pain medication to the patient on whom she projects her own pain or a nurse who does not give enough medication to the patient in pain because she is judging her own pain as a perceived weakness.

The administration may project blame onto midmanagement nurses, who then project their feelings of inadequacy and guilt onto staff members. Denial of our fear, shame, guilt, and inadequacy protects us from unacceptable feelings of vulnerability in a system that teaches us that it's not okay to feel, that we must be strong, good, right, and perfect.

Guilt

In her book *The Self-Sabotage Syndrome: Adult Children in the Workplace,* Janet Woititz describes guilt in an interview she held with a nurse manager. The manager commented, "Guilt is a wonderful motivator for nurses. Viewed by others as an angel of mercy and self-sacrificing, I learned that saying no was just not an acceptable way for me to deal with my limitations. Consequently, I became a skilled manipulator, deal maker, and controller of my environment. If these methods didn't work, my temper flared up: martyrdom and excuse-making would surely work" (1989:36).

Dishonesty

Dishonesty is another trait of an addictive system. It can be directed to oneself ("This policy is for the good of all my nurses, and my motives are for their interest"), to others ("We managers are not here to babysit the nursing staff!"), and to the world ("Our institution's only interest is to minister to the sick and needy.")

Broken Promises

Broken promises are characteristic of an addictive system. When a supervisor or director promises to take the staff's complaints to the administration and to report back to the group and then the nurses hear nothing more of the matter, feelings of abandonment, anger, and frustration arise. For the nurse who comes from an alcoholic or other dysfunctional family, these feelings may be intensified by unresolved childhood issues.

When asked in this author's survey if administration honored promises of salary raises, benefits, and better working conditions, 70 percent of the nurses questioned answered no. One nurse commented, "They usually change their minds, but that's life." A nurse who works in a federally operated hospital stated, "In the health care system, changes take so long. It's difficult to keep track of the promises, and I think this is used to the administration's advantage."

False promises keep people away from present issues because they focus on future expectations. They may be promises of a future pay raise, better working conditions, or an easier staffing schedule. A nurse stated that when she was hired, she was promised that she would be required to work nights only until the next daytime position opened up, within the year. She has been working nights for three years now, and two new people (new graduates who the head nurse felt required close supervision and instruction) have been hired for daytime slots .

Competition Between Peers

Competition is based on comparisons that make someone better than someone else. It is based on external referencing (looking to someone else to see how we are doing) and judging our performance by how it compares to someone else's. Peer reviews in an institution frequently use external referencing. The competency or success of a staff nurse may be measured by how the nurse compares with another nurse. The nurse may be required to deny the messages inside herself that tell her how she has performed.

Margaret worked per diem in a treatment center for chemical dependency and asked for an evaluation at the completion of her orientation. She was interested in communicating with the nurse manager those areas she felt comfortable in and those in which she required additional help.

When Margaret asked her manager how she felt the orientation had gone, the manager responded quickly, "Have you learned how to operate the glucometer yet?" Margaret felt as if she had been spied on, as if this head nurse knew her every move. The only way her manager could have known that Margaret had not used the glucometer was by privately speaking to the evening staff nurse with whom Margaret was orienting. The five-minute evaluation was focused on this one task, and Margaret left feeling confused, shamed, and inadequate. It took careful self-evaluation to affirm that she had given quality care to the patients, had read the procedure books, knew the policies, and had done an excellent job of learning the unit.

Snow and Willard (1989) state that performance evaluations must include the component of value for who you are and what you do to contribute your unique gifts to the unit. They have shown that performance evaluations frequently evaluate the nurse on everything except value. Shaming messages that say "do more" are not messages of a functional organization. They are the message that many of us grew up with: "I am not good enough."

THE ACOA EMPLOYEE IN AN
ADDICTIVE ORGANIZATION

Because a large number of health care employees are adult children of alcoholics (ACoAs), sabotage in the health care institution is common. Janet Woititz (1989:3-14) lists characteristics of adult children of alcoholics as they manifest in the workplace. These characteristics can provide valuable information for employee assistance programs:

• ACoAs are prime candidates for burnout. The excellent performance you admire and want has a limited life span.

- ACoAs tend not to know how to handle stress and lose more days due to illness than other employees.
- ACoAs are prone to depression, especially around holidays, so performance may lag at those times.
- ACoAs have difficulty with separation and change, so are prone to quit impulsively or do poorly with new opportunities.
- ACoAs run a higher risk of developing substance abuse problems than other employees.
- ACoAs don't know how to say no.
- ACoAs are frequently scapegoats.
- ACoAs lie when it would be just as easy to tell the truth.
- ACoAs judge themselves without mercy.
- ACoAs overreact to changes over which they have no control.
- ACoAs constantly seek approval and affirmation. They look for it in their supervisors and overwork in order to get strokes.
- ACoAs feel that they are different from other people. They may comply with requests even if they don't feel appropriate, because they don't want to be different.
- ACoAs are either super responsible or super irresponsible.
- ACoAs are extremely loyal, even when the loyalty is undeserved.

THE ACOA SUPERVISOR IN AN ADDICTIVE ORGANIZATION

Codependents and addicts may be put into supervisory roles of an addictive institution. According to

Woititz (1989:67), the following traits are characteristic of the ACoA supervisor:
- They demand compliance.
- They make changes overnight.
- They want to be liked by everyone.
- They give away their ego to the organization.
- They keep personal feelings under control.
- They have a need for perfection.
- They may become enablers.

Supervisory enabling, or institutional cobehavior, amplifies the individual nurse's dependency or codependency. Institutional cobehavior is filled with denial, shame, and control. Snow and Willard define professional codependence as: "Any act or behavior that shames and does not support the value, vulnerability, interdependence, level of maturity, and account-ability/spirituality of a nurse, patient, or colleague" (1989:141).

Enabling does not support the value, maturity, or accountability of a staff member. Supervisors and managers may enable their staff and cover up for the impaired nurse. Jane was a nurse aide who caused extreme problems on her unit with her unresolved family anger. She had an urgent need for approval from authority figures, especially mother roles. Her pattern was to win over a new supervisor with flowers, gifts, and cards. Once she had won the manager's affection, she would test her supervisor's loyalty by starting rumors about the staff and by complaining about her unit to other people in administrative positions.

Jane's supervisors - - the nurse practitioner, the head nurse, the chief nurse - - found it difficult to discipline Jane, and their avoidance of the problem enabled Jane to continue her behavior. The unit rapidly went through head nurses. Every time a head nurse became stressed enough to document Jane's behavior, she received no support from her supervisors. One of the head nurses who addressed the problem was ordered to dispose of all documentation that pointed to Jane's disruptive behavior.

Table 1, taken from Janet Woititz's book *The Self-Sabotage Syndrome*, reveals seven styles of addictive management and the codependent responses to them. These management styles are based on control, people pleasing, feelings of superiority, and fear.

TABLE 1

ADDICTIVE MANAGEMENT STYLES

Management Style	Codependent Response
Overcritical. Nothing is good enough. Praise is withheld.	"I want him/her to like me. Next time, I'll be good enough."
Overdemanding. Swamps self with work. Swamps employees with work. Expects it done in unrealistic time.	"He wouldn't ask me to do it if he didn't think I could do it. I'll prove I'm worthy."
The promiser.	"This time he means it."
Workaholic or incompetent.	"I need to take care of him."
Demeaning. "You're paranoid. You're making a big deal out of nothing. How can you be so stupid?"	"If I had his pressures I'd probably react the same way. He wouldn't say it if it weren't true."

Laissez-faire.	"If I were important enough, he'd pay more attention to me. If I don't have full and complete instructions, I'll screw up."
Rescuing.	"He will understand my pressures and problems, and I don't have to worry if I let certain things go."

Source: Janet Woititz, 1989.

CONCLUSION

Recovery from an addictive system begins with awareness of the problem. Education is the first step. Step one of the twelve-step programs states, "We admitted we were powerless over (our addictions) and that our lives had become unmanageable." Naming the problem is not judgement but rather an end of denial and a beginning of authenticity.

If we are to raise the system's consciousness, every member of the system must take responsibility. Mary Riley believes, "As long as even one of us thinks we are not a part of the problem of addictiveness, we are part of the problem." She adds, "Addictiveness cannot be understood intellectually only. When we are intellectual and point to the failings of others, we become a closed system. We use the weaknesses of others to deny our own feelings. A closed system does not see the truth. To understand addictive behaviors in others, we must understand our own truth" (1990:14).

CHAPTER SEVEN

PERSONAL RECOVERY:
JOURNEY TO AUTHENTICITY

RECOGNIZING THE NEED FOR HELP

Inflexibility, compulsive behaviors, poor communication patterns, and rescuing are all signs of a helper who needs help. Emotions become tightly controlled. Chronic negativity, anger, and depression result from repressing emotions. Ulcers, insomnia, low back pain, and other stress-related disorders are common in the nurse who needs recovery.

The need to be indispensable to our workplaces, our patients, our peers, and the doctors leads to grandiosity. Beliefs such as "I am the only one who can fix this situation, cure this patient, handle this doctor" are reinforced by cries of praise for professional codependence. When a nurse's professional self-esteem is directly linked to the patient's progress or to the success of the unit, the nurse becomes preoccupied with the illusion of control. Successes and failures are personalized. The nurse overidentifies with the patient and takes on too much responsibility. Burnout is just around the corner.

Carmen Renee Berry describes what she calls the Messiah Trap as the syndrome of gaining self-worth by helping others:

> We do not increase our value when we make other people happy, gain people's trust, or provide them with the things they need. Messiahs do not move up a notch on the 'worth' scale by giving to the poor, protecting the vulnerable, or rescuing those in crisis. Studying and grappling with complicated issues may increase understanding, but these efforts add nothing to a person's value. The causes for which you fight may be worthy, but they do not increase your worth (1988:84).

It is not possible to increase your self-worth through helping others. Acceptance of your inherent worth is a step in recovery.

The codependent nurse must ask herself, "What price am I paying for my codepencency? Do I feel burned out and stressed? Where am I in my relationship to drugs and alcohol? Am I happy in my work? Am I satisfied in my personal life? Am I hiding any addictive behaviors from my friends and peers? Does my institution support my well-being, or does it promote my codependency?" This assessment of whether life has become unmanageable because of codependency or addiction is the first step in recovery.

RECOVERY TOOLS

Learning Detachment

To be attached means to become overly involved and focused on others. For nurses, attachment may be a preoccupation with their patients. Nurses may worry about, talk about, call in about a patient, unable to cease thinking about the patient even when away from work. They may obsess about problems at work, planning their defense for the next staff meeting. Attachment is a reaction rather than a response.

To detach means to give others the freedom to grow through their own mistakes and experiences. It is not feeling responsible for others, but rather allowing others to learn self-responsibility. Pia Mellody says that we must put our emotional, mental, spiritual, and physical hands back in our own pockets and let people alone. [*] When we detach, we make a decision to care for ourselves rather than continually take care of others. The rewards of detachment include a wonderful release of burdens that leads to peace and serenity.

Breaking the Pattern

A task of learning to detach is removing oneself from the triangular involvement in what Berry refers to as the Victim/Offender/Rescuer (VOR) Response Pattern (1988: 91). This pattern of relating is present when there has been any form of abuse in a person's past and is used as a way to cope with the initial victimizing incident.

In the VOR Response Pattern, the Victim perceives herself or himself as powerless and deserving of abuse. The victim embraces the experience of victimization as a way to prevent change. Victims give their empowerment to others and feel that they are treated poorly because they are victims. Not only do victims allow abuse, they also often perpetuate it to take the focus of responsibility off of their own actions. Victims use abuse to keep from growing up.

The Offender perceives herself or himself as powerful over others and entitled to offend. By offending, the person avoids feelings of powerlessness. The offender also has been abused in the past and now denies the impact of the abuse by identifying with the role of the assailant. Like victims, offenders are reenacting the initial victimization experience, but they use abuse as a coverup for their pain. Offenders are addicted to victims.

The Rescuer, frequently seen in the nurse, attempts to cover up the initial victimization by perceiving herself or himself as a helper and caregiver of victims. By rescuing, rescuers can deny their own feelings of powerlessness of past experiences of abuse. Rescuers attempt to regain control by taking care of others. Of these three, rescuers or helpers play the most powerful role, because their actions appear purely selfless. Rescuers are addicted to helping. Instead of compulsively hurting, they compulsively help.

All three of these roles are attempts for control by a person who feels disempowered. The offender and the rescuer control the victim, and the victim controls the position of victimhood by allowing the abuse. We can actually switch positions in this triangle of interaction within one conversation. The following is a conversation in which each party takes turns around the VOR triangle:

> Leah is sitting on the couch. Daniel is sitting opposite her. Anger appears on Leah's face; Leah's jaw is tightly clenched. Her voice is low, trying to

find control. "You failed me again," she hisses (Offender). Daniel agrees. "I know I am screwing up," he pleads. "But let's talk about it" (Victim). Leah sits back, anger turning into hurt. "I can't stand this much longer," she cries. "It is so hard always to be the one left behind" (Victim). .... "There now, I'm here for you" Daniel coos (Rescuer). "Here for me? How can I ever trust you again!" Leah screams (Offender). " Oh, c'mon. It's not that big of a deal," Daniel shouts back (Offender)... (Summers, 1991:37)

To regain a sense of authentic power, people must acknowledge their past victimizations. They must realize that they are responsible only for their own behavior and allow others to take care of themselves. Breaking the VOR Response Pattern entails fostering self-care and esteem.

Setting Boundaries

Another task of learning to detach is setting boundaries. Boundaries are made with a sense of personal accountability and honor of self and others. Healthy relationships do not accommodate the violation of boundaries. Setting boundaries involves risk, since other people may not like the boundaries that are being set. These people might even leave the person who sets boundaries. Yet people who do not set boundaries are deserting themselves for the sake of the approval of others. People must learn to know their boundaries and notice what makes them feel comfortable or uncomfortable.

In recovery, *we* decide what *we* need and want. We determine our rights and act accordingly. We learn to set limits clearly and to let go of other people's reactions to our limits. We learn to ask for what we need or want and become willing to accept the no that might come after our request. No's can be seen as needed additional information. They need not be felt as personal rejections but as clear communication that empowers us to take care of our needs in another way. When we can accept the no's that frequently come, we can move into self-care with dignity. In this way, a no to a request actually brings freedom to move on.

Learning to say no is a major task in recovery. One cannot learn to say yes to self-love until one learns to say no to unhealthy situations. When the staffing office calls and puts pressure on a nurse to work a double shift, hinting that patients won't be cared for unless the nurse comes in, the nurse in recovery will check inside herself to determine whether she truly wants to help out or whether she would be reacting out of guilt. She will give herself permission to say, "I'm sorry, I have plans," regardless of what her plans are.

Berry states that helpers deserve the time and energy it takes to attend to themselves. She explains:

> It is time for us to break free of our overly serious approach to life and laugh, have fun, cultivate frivolity, and joy. We need to learn how to say 'Yes!' — to having fun, to going on adventures, to attending spiritual retreats, to spontaneous outings, to developing our artistic talents, to listening to music, to reading enjoyable books, to soaking in bubble baths, to exercising regularly, to filling our homes with cut flowers and beauty and art (1988:91).

Self-Care

By participating in recovery, we learn to ask, "What do I need to do to take care of myself today?" Self-care is a learned behavior that comes with practice. The tools of self-care are simple to use, but it is not always easy to remember to use them. Self-care cannot be accomplished without self-love. We need to ask ourselves if we feel worthy enough to care for ourselves, even as a priority over caring for others.

Carl Simonton, a leading cancer specialist, has identified some ways that cancer patients take care of themselves. He suggests meditation as a way to replenish their energy when they work hard as well as physical exercise and massage. He also stresses the importance of therapy and support groups. Frequent vacations are also important, as well as learning to ask for what you want and need. Dr. Simonton expresses his belief that if your work is interfering with your growth and pleasure, you must be willing to give it up. He believes in doing the work you love, whether it is approved of or not. These suggestions can be applied to anyone in any kind of recovery.

Support Groups

Professional recovery is not possible without personal recovery, and it is difficult to personally recover alone. Asking for help is one of the most difficult tasks a codependent helper can face, since asking for help requires admitting to vulnerability and risking rejection. A person who pretends not to be hurting will not ask for help and becomes needless and wantless (antidependent). Yet playing the role of being able to handle everything without help is lonely and frightening. To heal requires a safe place to become vulnerable.

When joining a recovery group, you will hear a message of hope within the safety of a nonjudgemental structure. You are assured that you will not be re-shamed when becoming vulnerable. It is difficult for professionals such as nurses to attend recovery programs where they may be recognized by a patient or client. Yet it is important to know that the nurse cannot continue to be in service for another in a healthy and functional way until she puts her own recovery first and submits to the commonality found in a support group.

In self-help groups such as CoDA, ACoA, AA, Al-Anon, and NA, nobody takes on the role of therapist or professional helper. This allows all members, regardless of occupation, to come together as equals who are participating in and witnessing the healing of everyone there. The nurse who is afraid of seeing a patient will be surprised at a meeting when her patient welcomes her, expressing continued trust and support for her as a professional. In fact, the nurse may find that the patient actually will trust more, knowing that the helper is helping herself.

Specialty support groups and organizations are also available to the nurse in recovery. A list of resources for help was included in Chapter 5 and contains the National Consortium of Chemical Dependency Nurses, International Nurses Anonymous, and the National Nurses Society on Addictions. You might also look for a local CODA group specifically for those in helping professions.

Onsite support groups are becoming visible, and the nurse or other employee must be assured his or her anonymity when attending meetings. She must be given the opportunity to attend meetings either during breaks, at lunchtime, or before or after work. She must also be comfortable that she will not be judged by her supervisor or punished on her job evaluation because she has sought help.

Adequate support from employee assistance programs for personal recovery is imperative. Personal recovery must be treated as an asset rather than a disability. Studies show that people who have come from a dysfunctional family system make much better employees when in recovery: sick leaves decline and physical health and well-being increase as past psychosomatic illnesses lessen. An alcoholic or chemically dependent nurse who is in recovery will be aware of self-care and will therefore be a functional part of the system.

FEELINGS

As people working in a stressful profession, nurses often lose touch with their own feelings. Many nurses are able to identify others' feelings better than they can their own. They may have stuffed feelings down inside in order to survive daily exposure to trauma and suffering. They may have been afraid that their feelings would become overwhelming if they acknowledged them. They may have felt they were above having feelings. Yet, recovery starts only when one can feel one's desperation, anger, exhaustion, and fear.

To move from dysfunctional service to authentic service, nurses must recover their feelings. They may have repressed emotions for so long that it is difficult to even identify a feeling that they are experiencing. Often a person will repress a feeling such as anger because it feels unacceptable, fearful, and shameful. The person will then substitute a more acceptable emotion such as sadness.

I recall sitting in a therapist's office, crying softly, expressing what I thought was the feeling of sadness. I just sat there and wept. The therapist asked me, "What are you feeling right now?" I tried to tune into the authentic feeling, but I had no idea what it was. I was using my weeping as an acceptable front and was totally out of touch with my true feeling! I sat for a long time, dabbing my eyes with a handkerchief, then admitted that I could not identify the feeling. My therapist asked, "Could you possibly be feeling anger?" I did not even know what anger felt like! We worked together on anger, beating pillows. I learned that I had repressed my anger and substituted sadness, which was an acceptable and familiar expression that I had learned in my family of origin.

In recovery we acknowledge and accept our feelings. We learn that what we are feeling is valid, that we have no reason to feel guilty for our feelings. Feelings are neither good nor bad. They do not have to be explained in an attempt to make someone else understand them. In fact, we cannot demand from anyone to understand our feelings, only to accept them as real for us. The feeling process has three parts: *feel, deal, and reveal.*

Feeling the Feeling

The first phase of the feeling process — to feel the feeling — is necessary to know what to do with the feeling. We need to take time to acknowledge the sensation, uncensored, unblocked. What does it taste like? What color is it? What does it look like? We can write about the feeling, draw it, dance it, sing it, shout it!

Obsession is a dysfunctional tool designed to avoid feeling. It is a function of the mind, not of the heart. For example, when someone obsesses about a relationship at work or at home, planning the next move or strategy to get back at another person, that person may be trying to avoid feeling the sadness of loneliness or the rage of a betrayal. Obsession is a defense mechanism against pain.

Journal writing can be beneficial in working with this phase of the feeling process. It can help us to understand repeated patterns. When we can write about our feelings of powerlessness, fear, anger, and unmanagability, we claim those feelings in the safety of our journal. We can see the point of helpless abyss, what I call our black sun, where we can finally feel the authentic pain. A journal helps us to be creative in our pain. The following is an example of a journal entry:

> Wrapped in my winter shawl, I sit and rock. The fire is burning, yet my body shivers. The moon is shining through my window, yet I see only darkness. Alone, I sit and rock. The stillness is deafening, yet I dread even the smallest sound, which seems to explode into my head, sending the last threads of sanity into painful chaotic vibration.... Sick, with fear and loneliness, I question all of my past choices and motives.... Filled with fear and insanity and self-doubt, I feel defenseless and defeated.... I am tired and weak.... I gather my shawl around my shoulders as I watch the embers dying in the fireplace.... Death feels welcome when compared to my waking state of agony.... I fall into my despair (Summers, 1991:111).

Can you feel the pain here? As we acknowledge our pain and the reality of our dysfunction, we touch our authenticity. Touching this authenticity will change us forever. When we have accepted the pain within, experiencing the intensity of our feelings, those feelings must be honored. We will cry. We will feel the truth of our wounds.

Dealing with the Feeling

Only after we know what the feeling is do we begin to examine the thoughts that accompany the feeling. Once we have identified a feeling, we can acknowledge it, thank it, and affirm to ourselves that we no longer have to be controlled by it. This second phase of the feeling process is where we deal with the feeling by examining it and exploring its origin. An extreme reaction to an event may be a trigger feeling — an old feeling triggered by a new situation. For example, if my supervisor were to say to me, "I have to talk to you about something that is bothering me, but now is not a good time," I may identify the trigger feeling of fear, even terror. When I move into dealing with the feeling — identifying the feeling's origin — I may find that the statement has triggered a memory I have as a frightened child when I was made to wait in my room with no information about what was going on, wondering whether I had done something to cause my parents to fight or drink. This memory brings back the feeling of powerlessness. Now, aware of the origin of the feeling, I can deal with the feeling intellectually, knowing that it has little to do with what is presently going on.

Revealing the Feeling

It is in the third phase of the feeling process that I reveal my feeling, being careful to use "I" messages. I take responsibility for my feeling with no need to apologize for it. I do not blame as I communicate my feeling. Rather than say, "You made me feel

_____," I will say, "I felt _____ when you
_____." Therefore, when my supervisor says that
she must talk to me later, I can respond rather than react:
"When you allude that there may be a problem that we
must talk about later, I feel uncomfortable about the wait.
Could we talk about it briefly now so that I don't have to
spend my day wondering what it is about?"

Anger

Often we carry old tapes or codependent rules about
anger. We may believe that it is not acceptable to feel
angry. We may fear that we will lose control or that
people will abandon us if we express our anger. We may
fear that if someone becomes angry with us, the person
will stop loving us.

As we enter recovery, it is common to experience
intense anger. As we acknowledge our wounds
throughout life, the times we have been victimized or
abused, the lies we were told as a child, the years of
trying to help everyone in a desperate attempt to get love,
anger will arise. Anger that is released inappropriately,
either at work or at home, can be very destructive.
However, if we do not feel, deal with, and reveal our
anger, the anger may grow into resentment. The Big Book
of Alcoholics Anonymous states, "... this business of
resentment is infinitely grave. We found that it is fatal.
For when harboring such feelings we shut ourselves off
from the sunlight of the Spirit" (AA, 1976:66). Saint
Thomas expressed the importance of acknowledging
anger when he stated, "Anger is harmless. We need to
guard against revenge, retaliation, and resentment."
These are the results of unattended anger.

Hiding behind the walls of anger is fear. Gary Zukav
explains that behind all fear is a sense of powerlessness:

You lose power when you rage against an injustice. You lose power when you are threatened by another person, or other people. You lose power when you distance yourself from your fellow humans out of resentment or bitterness, or a sense of disappointment or unworthiness or superiority. Beneath all of these is fear, fear that you are vulnerable, that you are not able to cope without the person or situation that you miss, that you are at a disadvantage without that which you envy (1989:223).

Anger is part of the healing process. It is a signal that needs to be paid attention to. Anger may signify that our rights are being violated, that we are in an abusive relationship, or that we have given too much of ourselves away to someone else. Anger is inevitable when we are constantly placed in a submissive role or when we take on too much responsibility for others. Through anger, we may get in touch with injustices. Anger carries an incredible amount of energy. It is the release of overflowing frustration. But we must learn how to deal with anger constructively rather than destructively.

In her book *The Dance of Anger,* Harriet Lerner describes the difference between *feeling* anger and *venting* anger. Feeling anger signals the problem, but venting anger does not solve it. Lerner states, "Venting anger may serve to maintain, and even rigidify, the old rules and patterns in a relationship, thus ensuring that change does not occur" (1985:4). When we are venting anger, we are not working on change. We are too busy defending and offending to present a clear statement.

Raging is a reaction to feelings of powerlessness and

helplessness. An interaction occurs when one person, perhaps a screaming nurse, strikes out in an aggressive power play. The nurse may actually be helping others in the interaction to stay calm in a balancing act of sorts. When one rages, the other looks good and feels calm. This may create more rage as a result of feeling not heard or feeling ashamed. When a person's shame core has been triggered, the person has a shame attack. The reaction may be more rage, then more fear and shame, then more rage, while the other person becomes more calm and emotionally cool. This cycle needs to be broken.

Managing Anger

Lerner (1985:10) describes three styles of managing anger that are disempowering:

1. silent submission
2. ineffective fighting and blaming
3. emotional distancing

Submission and blame are, respectively, passive and aggressive behavior. When neither of these methods works, a reaction of survival will often be experienced as emotional distancing. For example, a nurse who is meek and cannot stand up to a physician or supervisor when requested to perform a menial task, screams at the doctor, "Are your hands tied? Call for your own labs!" and finally shrugs and walks away, distancing emotionally by feeling, "What's the use anyway?"

Anger is an emotion which is energy in motion. Using the fiery energy of anger can be productive and empowering. But anger can be like having a tiger by the tail: if we are not prepared to move from a balanced position, our own anger may attack us. Lerner (1985:13-

14) lists four areas to develop when working with anger:

1. Tune in to the source of the anger, clarify your position.
2. Learn communication skills.
3. Observe and stop nonproductive patterns of interaction.
4. Learn to anticipate and deal with reactions from others.

Lerner's book *The Dance of Anger* is for anyone who experiences passive or aggressive patterns in his or her interactions. The book offers tools to develop empowering interactions while utilizing the energy of anger and lists the goals of utilizing anger productively:

> First, "letting it all hang out" may not be helpful. Second, the only person we can change and control is our own self. Third, changing our own self can feel so threatening and difficult that it is often easier to continue an old pattern of silent withdrawal or ineffective fighting and blaming. And, finally, de-selfing is at the heart of our most serious anger problems (Lerner, 1985:40).

De-selfing is losing self while in relationship with others. It is a form of self abuse. It is giving away our identity and value to others when under pressure. De-selfing creates tremendous anger, and that anger is often projected onto the perceived offender. The anger is actually at ourself for defining our identity and value from the perception of another.

We can learn to translate anger into clear, concise, and nonjudgemental statements about self instead of expressions of tears, screaming, guilt, helplessness, or confusion. Lerner states, "Anger is a tool for change when it challenges us to become more of an expert on the self and less of an expert on others" (1985:102).

HEALING THE PAST

In recovery, we explore the origins of our dysfunctional patterns. Before we are able to do so, however, we must perceive and accept those patterns as character defects. It is easy to overlook a negative trait in ourselves and not so easy to perceive a positive trait that is carried to an extreme as a character defect (such as helping carried to an extreme becoming enabling). Some patterns are difficult to identify and claim. Our friends, families, and patients can serve us in discovering our own traits by reflecting back that which we have not become aware of. This is what I call Mirror Work: we learn to take whatever we judge in another and turn the mirror around to view it in ourselves. This concept is stated poetically in a line from a song by Jai Josefs entitled I Love Myself the Way I Am": "I love the world the way it is 'cause I can clearly see, that all the things I judge are done by people just like me.... (Jai Josefs, 1983 Jai-Jo Music.)

After we have identified the pattern and claimed it as our own, we must be willing to take it to its origin. When did our feelings and insecurities first occur? When did we feel unsafe and begin to use survival strategies? When did we first feel powerless and out of control of our environment? When did we stop trusting?

Snow and Willard speak of the importance of finding the origin of patterns:

Those things that aren't working in our lives relate directly to things we experienced or were taught in our families of origin. Without remembering, it is impossible to dispute the early messages about our value and rules for life that haven't worked — values and rules we embrace and function from as adults that compromise integrity, truth, authenticity, intimacy, and inner peace (1989:85).

The Wounded Child

At the core of each dysfunctional pattern lives a wounded child. In recovery, we complete the emotional business of our childhood. We look at what happened in our past, grieve our losses, and learn to let go. If we want to release the past, we must uncover the family secrets that we were never allowed to tell. This is a good time to go into therapy with a therapist who knows the family systems approach to recovery. At the same time, we can benefit by participating in support groups, such as twelve-step programs (CoDA for codependency and Adult Children of Alcoholics are excellent programs for healing childhood wounds). Support groups provide a safe place for people to process without fear of judgement or ridicule. Also, a number of excellent self-help workbooks are available (see Suggested Readings) that one can use as an adjunct to therapy and support group attendance.

Recovery from a difficult past involves learning to reparent ourselves. We become the parent to our wounded child that we never had. We help ourselves to grow in the safe, nonabusive environment of self-love. Reparenting requires tools that must be learned before we can work with our wounded child. We must be gentle with ourselves and get the help we need so as to not further abuse ourselves or others.

Forgiveness

Healing the past requires forgiveness. Emmet Fox was once heard to say that by holding resentments against another person, you are bound to that person by a cosmic link; you are mentally chained to the one you resent. Resentment is a bond stronger than steel. I have also heard that forgiveness is giving up all hope for a better yesterday.

The process of forgiveness has three steps. The first step is to *own the feeling* . If you are angry or hurt, you must first recognize the feeling. Giving the feeling a name is the first step required for working with it. You cannot release anything if you are unaware that you have it. Remember that emotions are energy in motion. Owning anger puts the feeling in motion rather than allowing it to settle in the pit of your stomach, turning slowly into resentment.

The second step in the process of forgiveness is to *release the feeling*. We have to learn to let go of the pain, the anger, the hostility. The simple phrase "I would have preferred" might help this process. I would have preferred the past to be different, but it was not. I am now ready to let it go. A minister once spoke of forgiveness as a process of letting go of an emotion that we have grown to love and need. He explained that to forgive fully, a person must be willing to give up his or her most cherished wound.

A woman had struggled with letting go of her anger over the death of her teenage son by a drunken driver. She was full of hatred, which had lasted for over a year. She wanted to forgive, but she could not. Her anger was controlling her life. Every time she was about to release it, she took it back again. Finally, she fell on her knees and prayed: "God, I can't forgive him. Forgive me, God, for not being able to forgive him." Her forgiveness started at this instant when she was able to release her anger to God.

The third step in the process of forgiveness is *acceptance* . We need to learn to accept people the way they are. We cannot forgive completely without this step. We may find that the most loving thing we can do in the process of forgiveness is to accept the situation and, in our own self-love, leave it. Love by definition cannot be conditional. Relating *is* conditional. It is not self-loving to accept and to remain in an abusive situation. However, it is loving of self and others to accept the situation, determine whether it is worth the stress of staying, and do something about it if possible or leave it if it is not likely to change. This, of course, applies to both personal and work situations.

CHOICES: A GIFT OF RECOVERY

In recovery, inevitable questions will come up for the nurse: Is my job appropriate for my self-care? Why do I stay if I am miserable? Is the institution where I work capable of hearing and honoring my needs? Am I putting myself in an abusive situation each day that I come to work? What will I do if I leave? Can I make it on my own? Do I have what it takes to go out there and stand on my own? Dysfunctional questions may also arise: Who will need me if I quit being a nurse? Can I find satisfaction when not saving a life? How will I look good?

As we become clear with our motives and strengths, our weaknesses and vulnerabilities, we may decide that our institution is not good for us or that nursing is not appropriate for us anymore. In the book *The Addictive Organization*, Anne Wilson Schaef and Diane Fassel state that if organizations continue to function dysfunctionally, their best people will fall away. The most highly motivated men and women, who contribute much to an organization and are willing to devote time and energy, will leave. Schaef and Fassel explain, "The single-minded pursuit of profit, coupled with addictive behavior, left these employees with a sense of moral exhaustion and deterioration. For the most part, they decided they could not change the company by themselves, but they could take responsibility for their own lives. Most left the organization" (1988:209).

If you decide to leave nursing, you may experience guilt and confusion: Why am I no longer able to be a good and loyal nurse? What will the other nurses think of me? You may feel guilty for abandoning others when you "should" stay and help. But by moving into your unique position of authenticity, you will serve in your own personal ways. In sharing your process, whether deciding to leave or stay, you can exemplify the courage of someone who is acknowledging self-love by following her bliss.

Judith Duerk describes the feelings behind choosing to leave a service career like nursing:

> I was leaving with great sorrow, even though I knew I could not grow into myself if I remained. Leaving behind the hearkening to outer authority to find my own meaning. Leaving behind the clarity and comfort of having my duty defined from outside. Leaving behind projecting my leadership ability onto others instead of owning it myself. Leaving behind being a "good woman" in

service to others. Forced, now, to claim my energy to serve the Self as I interpreted it. Forced to become, on my own terms, who I truly was, to be willing to suffer my guilt against the collective for becoming myself (1989).

If you decide to leave nursing, you may experience judgement from your peers, who might say, "She can't take the pressure" or "How could she leave when we need nurses so badly?" You must be careful not to judge former peers for judging you. We often project our own guilt of leaving onto our peers. When I left the field of active nursing, my fear of abandonment was mirrored for me. I thought they thought I was abandoning them, when my fear was that if I didn't take care of myself, *I* would be abandoning *me*.

My total identity at the time of my departure from active nursing was that of registered nurse. Who was I if I wasn't a nurse? What will I do if people are not depending on my skills to survive? Yet when I began to practice my own self-love, I developed the courage to change what I could. And what I could change were the situations I had put myself in that did not feel good to me anymore. I finally accepted that if I did not quit — at least temporarily — I would lose myself completely.

When asked how she left nursing, Deborah explained that she resisted the break for years until the choice was made for her: "I got real sick! I was forced to leave nursing. Later I tried to come back. I wanted to take care of people again. But I was literally bombarded by my patients' distresses. I got a real education concerning why I got sick in the first place. I had to leave again, this time chemically dependent as well as codependent. I had to finally tell myself that it was okay not to be a nurse."

It is not always necessary to quit nursing. It may be enough to take a temporary break from it for a while to try something different. Whether we choose to stay in nursing or leave, it is important to understand that *we* determine wherever *we* go and whatever *we* do.

There are many options within nursing. It is an expansive profession. Positions within nursing range from education to specialty areas. Nurses can work in the field of counseling, consultation, or holistic health. There are many nursing entrepreneurial areas being developed, and nurses are creating their own businesses. New techniques such as "Touch for Health" are being developed to augment traditional nursing. Writing this book has been a way for me to serve by sharing my experience, hope, and strength. By helping myself, I develop a more expanded concept of helping others. There is a global service that happens when we help ourselves. When we become empowered in our own recovery, we can give from the heart, not from the need to give for the ego's sake.

Some nurses who choose to leave will eventually choose to reenter the profession. Many have described their struggle with illusion as they return to find the same problems and experience the same frustrations with an old system. Many find it easier to enter a different field of nursing.

Nurses reentering the profession have an opportunity to bring a new awareness to nursing. One nurse offers words of advice to those considering reentry: "Know what you are willing to do, what limitations you have. Know how to say no. Make a commitment to stick to your needs." This recovering nurse has learned self-care. Now, when asked to do more than her share, she looks inside herself for a response. She checks her motives and makes sure she is not falling into the addiction of needing to be needed. She reviews her boundaries.

Another nurse chose to return to nursing because of her love for service. Pamela is actively involved in her recovery and is now nursing from an empowered perspective:

> Although I have done my share of complaining, nursing has been a mainstay in my life. I know what being burned out is like, and I have learned ways to avoid it. I still try to give a high standard of care, but it is not my main priority in life anymore. I've had to learn that it's okay to take care of myself, to recuperate from an illness, to not work extra shifts if I have something planned. In the end, I am a better person and nurse for doing these things. I have come to respect other nurses that do the same for themselves, instead of looking down on them for not helping out more. I think nursing is a wonderful profession if you can view it realistically and balance it with your personal life.

RECOVERY: TRANSFORMING PAST WOUNDS INTO PRESENT GEMS

As an irritating grain of sand becomes a pearl when the oyster accepts it as a part of the whole, past wounds will become our unique gifts to ourselves and to the world when we accept them and work with them in recovery. Robert Ackerman, author of *Perfect Daughters*, states that childhood lessons are both liabilities and assets (1989: 97). Our painful experiences can be transformed into useful qualities such as perseverance, courage, and intuition (see Table I).

TABLE 1:

CHILDHOOD LESSONS

Enacted as Dysfunctions	Transformed to qualities
If I can control everything, I can keep my family from being upset.	I am a survivor. I can survive.
If I please everyone, everyone will be happy.	I have developed competencies in many areas in my life.
It is my fault, and I am to blame when trouble occurs.	I can handle crisis.
Those who love you the most are those who cause you the most pain.	I have a good sense of empathy.
If I don't get close emotionally, you cannot hurt me.	I can take care of myself.
It is my responsibility to see that everyone gets along with each other.	I am not easily discouraged.
Take care of others first.	I can find alternatives to problems.
Nothing is wrong, but I don't feel right.	I am not afraid to rely on my abilities.
Expressing anger is not appropriate.	I can be healthy when others are not.
Something is missing in my life.	I do have choices.
I'm unique and my family is different from all other families.	I can be depended upon.

I can deny anything.	I appreciate my inner strength.
I am not a good person.	I am a good person.
I am responsible for the success of a relationship.	I know what I want.
For something to be acceptable, I must be perfect.	I may not be perfect, but parts of me are great.

If you are working on recovery, if you have looked within, detached, faced the past, and learned self-care tools, you will be able to distill your experiences into a personal understanding of yourself. It is from this point of integration that you can develop ways of life that are not based on past character defects and coping patterns. Everything that you learn in recovery is going to appear in your future work and your relationships.

Addiction and Recovery

Addiction is not about which drug or which relationship or which job or which obsession we have chosen to be the focus of our attention. It is about finding something — anything — that helps us hide from our wounds, our pain, our joys, our personal truths. It is about running from our god-given lessons; refusing to see what we see, to feel what we feel; refusing to live our lives to the fullest. Addiction is about fear: fear of our vulnerabilities, fear of being shamed, fear of getting hurt, fear of being alone. Addiction is also about fear of our strengths and talents, even of our personal power.

Recovery is not about abstaining from substances or processes for the rest of our lives. It is not about sacrificing that glass of wine at dinner or abstaining from sex for the next five years, although these may be the *choices* we make in recovery. Recovery is not about giving up service to others for the sake of learning to say no. Recovery is not a prison of self-imposed limitations. Statements such as "I just can't do that anymore because I'm in recovery" are as restricting as the addictive substance or process that we are giving up.

When we truly find our authentic selves in recovery, when we begin to love ourselves and find our purposes from this love, we will put the fear of addiction behind us once and for all (fear of addiction is an addiction itself). We will become free to choose what is good for us. We will use the wisdom we have gained from our experiences to choose what to leave behind and what to now cultivate in our lives.

Recovery is not about "can't." It is about freedom. Freedom to talk about our addictions without shame, without fear of being criticized for our past behavior. Freedom to say we are scared or confused. Freedom to ask for help. Freedom to give help. Freedom to hold another who is afraid and to share our recovery. Freedom to experiment with life. Freedom to make mistakes.

Recovery is about accepting that we've made mistakes, for in every supposed failure there is success, a lesson that makes us stronger and wiser. When we give ourselves the freedom to talk about our mistakes, we discover their gifts. It is in this process that we find the choice to not repeat our mistakes and to move toward our successes with grace and ease rather than with surprise and awkwardness.

Recovery is about living life to its fullest. It is about self- responsibility. It is about being responsible for each personal transformation and then using that transformation as a tool for the next transformation. Chapter 8 discusses such a transformation: the recovery of an institution.

The rest of the book looks at some methods to integrate personal and professional recovery into the workplace of hospitals and institutions.

*Taped lecture by Pia Mellody, "Addictive Relationships," 1990.

CHAPTER EIGHT

INSTITUTIONAL RECOVERY:
HELP FOR THE HELPERS

THE NEED FOR HELP

An institution that has been focused on healing others may find it difficult to recognize itself as being in need of healing. It may help to understand the need for healing by using the family systems theory, which states that if an individual is sick, the entire family is sick. We work in a professional family made up of helpers. In their booklet entitled "Enabling in the Health Professions," Linda Crosby and LeClair Bissel explain that the professional family is similar to the nuclear family (father, mother, children) and is committed to maintaining an image for outsiders. Crosby and Bissel state:

> The general public, namely those we serve, has traditionally viewed the helping professions as special. We have obligations imposed on us because we belong to this prestigious group: We must adhere to the practice statutes of licensure,

conform to the image of our profession created by
the public, and protect that image from harm
(1991:14)

Crosby and Bissel explain that when the family image
is threatened, the professional family will band together,
hiding unacceptable behaviors from public view. This is
typical of any dysfunctional family that operates from the
rules that demand the family members to look good and
not talk about their problems. It is indicative of the
codependent behavior called enabling. Crosby and Bissel
state:

> While the nuclear family acts as a total system
> in the enabling process, it's comprised of one or
> more enablers. This also holds true for the helping
> professions. A total profession enables collectively
> through its organizations and institutions, but
> individual practitioners, supervisors, partners,
> and administrators enable within these
> organizations and institutions (1991:15).

Enabling is a codependent behavior based on the
denial of problems. Denial is indicative of an addictive
organization. Denial must be removed before recovery
can be initiated. Recovery for an individual or for an
entire institution is not a quick fix. It is a new way of life
that entails embracing new ideas, forming new habits,
and making difficult changes. When a dysfunctional
healing institution is in recovery, it can be transformed
into an authentic healing institution, one day at a time,
over a long period of time. Awareness of the problem is
the first step in recovery. Awareness comes from a close
scrutiny of addictive processes, both in the individual and

within the institution's structure. The next step is a sincere desire by the organization to go to any lengths to achieve recovery.

When a group of individuals within the institution are recovering, institutional recovery is also possible. But can the institution recover as a whole? Can the organization shift away from dysfunctional patterns and become a supportive and safe place for individuals to recover? What are the effects of group events, such as a transformational recovery program, on the lives of the people within that group? What comes first — individual recovery or institutional recovery?

In twelve-step programs we hear the goals of individual recovery — to become happy, joyous, and free. The goals of institutional recovery are similar: to provide safety, respect, open-mindedness, flexibility, and freedom for creativity.

This chapter discusses recovery tools that can be embraced by the health care institution — tools that have proven effective for the individual that may now be applied to the group. It offers suggestions for transformation of the institution and requires the cooperation of management. Recall four of the unwritten rules in a dysfunctional family: Be strong. Be good. Be right. Be perfect. These rules must be eliminated before an institution can begin recovery, for recovery requires an admission to being vulnerable and fallible.

WHAT HAS BEEN TRIED

Many management techniques have been tried in the workplace; among them are participatory management, shared governance, and democratic leadership. These techniques all suggest that the groups incorporating them are already functioning at a high, self-actualized level. The following paragraphs contain descriptions of quality circles, shared governance, unions, and training programs that may present sound ideas for a healthy institution. The techniques described in the following paragraphs require the members of the group to exhibit the same traits that are the goals for institutional recovery: safety, respect, open-mindedness, flexibility, and freedom for creativity. These techniques cannot be used as substitutes for a recovery program in the addictive organization. They will be successful only for the organization that is in recovery.

Quality Circles

William Ouchi developed Theory Z, a management style called the Quality Circle, where employees participate in all decision-making processes. The quality circle is based on the round-table principle, wherein team members sit together, discuss problems and solutions, and make decisions based on group conscience. Everyone takes responsibility for the results in an attempt to bring interdependency to the workplace.

Shared Governance

In a series of articles, Fay Bower (1990, 1991) contends that interdependency within the nursing profession has been difficult to achieve because nursing has functioned in a bureaucratic hierarchy. Bower describes the concept of shared governance, which is based on the belief that if management shares its power and decision making, nursing staffs will feel more autonomous and will operate at a higher level of efficiency.

Bower states, "Nurses in shared governance

frameworks do not just participate in decisions about their practice, they own their practice. Nurses belong to key decision-making groups and deal with issues of practice, quality of care, personnel issues" (1991:30).

A few of the components of shared governance include staff-and-management-determined nursing parameters; peer election of nurse leaders; peer review and accountability; absence of manager veto power; bylaws that have been developed by both staff and manager groups; nursing positions on the board of trustees; and staff determination of wages, budgets, staffing, and quality of work.

Bower describes the responsibility of shared governance as one that requires "an attitude and a willingness to be accountable for the kind and quality of nursing practice developed and delivered. Each nurse must be concerned with all that occurs and must be willing to confront, evaluate and censor those who do not meet standards" (1991:31).

Although these concepts are theoretically sound, serious problems may arise if the participants are codependents or addicts. Dysfunctional participants may bring their individual dysfunctions to the circle or shared governance system. When a codependent nurse is expected to confront and evaluate her/his peers who do not meet standards, participants may experience control issues, and chaos (the familiar state in a dysfunctional family) is inevitable. Problems are invented, because drama and confusion are functions of the addictive system.

Unions

The union is an organization that has offered to relieve the frustration of employees who work in a dysfunctional system without addressing the primary dysfunction of codependency. Unions support victimization with righteous exclamations of how the employees have been abused. Unions make false promises for a quick fix to the employees' miseries. Unions promise external rather than authentic power. They direct the employees' focus outward, depending on the employees for conflict resolution, suggesting that the employee is not able to explore the origins of the problem and become responsible for the solution.

Training Programs

Training programs and communications workshops have been tried with limited success, because they bring a false illusion of hope into the workplace. Some hospitals offer stress management programs to their employees in an attempt to reduce stress and increase productivity. Yet the primary issues of codependency, chemical dependency, and other addictive behaviors are not addressed, because it is not acceptable to be a member of a dysfunctional family.

RECOVERY

The very job description of a helper fosters and encourages codependency. As a result, recovery from codependency in a helping setting is a challenge. It is not helpful to point fingers and diagnose others as codependent. Recovery is a self-motivated program that invites all to participate.

For healing to occur, members of the institution must have a safe environment in which to seek help. A safe environment gives one the freedom to be vulnerable, to make mistakes, and to admit the need for help. To begin recovery, both the employer and the employee must be offered a healing environment in which to discover their addicitive patterns. A healing environment offers education, treatment of individual addictions, scrutiny of policies, twelve-step programs, emplyee assistance programs, and outside consultants.

Education

Since education is the key to recovery, the first essential step in recovery is education for self-identification through, for example, educational series on topics of codependency, adult children of alcoholics, and the addictive process. The family systems approach (i.e., perceiving the institution as a family where individuals learn patterns to exist and survive within the system) can be helpful in identifying the roles each member has chosen to play. Weekly inservices for health care providers that describe codependency and provide written materials could address the follwing topics:

- What is addiction?
- What are the components of the addictive system?
- What is codependency?
- Where did it come from?
- What role do I play in the system?
- How do I recover?

Treatment of Individual Addictions

To allow an employee with chemical dependency to continue to work unchecked is codependent. Any denial of individual addictions must be broken, and intervention for chemically impaired employees must be initiated in a nonjudgemental, nonpunitive way. Treatment must be offered in an in-patient facility when appropriate and twelve-step program information made available.

Scrutiny of Policies

Snow and Willard (1989) advise careful scrutiny of all nursing policies and procedures for issues of codependency, assessing to determine whether the values of both staff members and patients are supported within the policies. Checking for undertones of shame, disrespect, and unrealistic demands for conformity is a part of such an evaluation. A policy that is rigid, controlling, or unclear denies the opportunity for self-accountability. Evaluation criteria must also be assessed for areas of shaming, blaming, and judging.

The Twelve Steps of Recovery

For institutional recovery to be successful, both management and the employees need to be participating in the recovery process. It is essential that management commit to a program of recovery while supporting the employees' individual recovery programs. In this way, everyone can learn the commonality of being individuals who are joining in a collective transformation.

Group sessions, goal setting, development of plans, and careful followup are important tools for the organization that chooses to follow a recovery program. It is useful to have an employee assistance manager who is working an individual program of recovery and can support the group process. An outside consultant can function as a mediator for the institution until the program becomes familiar to the organization.

The twelve steps are another tool for the recovering organization. Table 1 lists Mary Riley's version of a twelve-step program for the workplace. The program was adapted from the twelve steps that have aided many individuals in recovering from alcoholism, narcotics addiction, eating disorders, nicotine addiction, gambling or sex addiction, and codependency, among other dysfunctions. The first step of Riley's recovery program is "We addmitted we were powerless over {whatever addiction} and our productiveness has decreased because of it" (Riley, 1990:48). This is a powerful step for an organization to take. To admit powerlessness may seem weak, but the strength actually comes in the disclosure that help is needed.

TABLE 1

12-STEP PROGRAM IN THE WORKPLACE

1. We admitted we were powerless over {whatever addiction} and our productiveness has decreased because of it.

2. We came to accept that we do not currently know everything we could know about our jobs.

3. We made a decision to accept the guidance of one other in the organization who is more familiar with the job.

4. We made a searching and fearless moral inventory of ourselves.

5. We admitted to ourselves and to another human being the exact nature of our sabotaging behavior on the job.

6. We were entirely ready to listen to the guidance and, for a moment, to let go of our original viewpoint.

7. Acknowledged the guidance, summarized it; asked questions to further understand it; said "thank you" and agreed to undertake the suggestion.

8. Made a list of all the persons we had harmed and became willing to

make amends to them, to others or to the corporation.

9. Made direct amends to such people whenever possible except when to do so would injure them or others.

10. Continued to take personal inventory and when we were wrong, promptly admitted it.

11. We are now safe to let our entrepreneurial spirit come back to life.

12. Having recaptured our entrepreneurial spirit, we carried this message to others whom we saw imprisoned in resistance to their own productiveness and creativity.

Source: Riley, 1990; p. 109.

The twelve-step recovery program is a spiritual program, and Mary Riley defines spirituality in the workplace as "the entrepreneurial spirit, the part of us that really wants to make a difference, to create, to be good in our work" (1990:47). The following is a summary of Riley's adaptation of the twelve steps of recovery in the workplace.

Step 1: "We admitted we were powerless over {whatever addiction} and our productiveness has decreased because of it." This is the time when we stop playing victim or martyr, we realize that our institution is experiencing problems arising from dysfunctional patterns, and we ask for help. In admitting that we may be a part of the problem, we can join in the solution.

Step 2: "We came to accept that we do not currently know everything we could know about our jobs." We become humble enough to accept help, to stop functioning under the dysfunctional rule "Be perfect," and to open our minds and hearts to learning.

Step 3: "We made a decision to accept the guidance of one other in the organization who is more familiar with the job." When we see someone who seems to be working an effective program of recovery, we can ask this person to be a mentor. Mentors function in the role of what recovery programs call sponsors, people who serve as healthy models and who are willing to share their own experience with others who want to grow. These are people who do not try to make you believe that they know more than you. Rather, they project a personal style of "walking their talk," being open to learning and growing themselves. Sponsors remind us of the tools available and guide us through the steps. People who have worked the steps in other organizations might become temporary sponsors until employees find someone in their own workplace to whom they can relate.

Step 4: "We made a searching and fearless moral inventory of ourselves." This is a step of courage, for it requires us to become vulnerable so that we can find out who we really are. The honesty that is asked of us may be difficult when we have been blaming others for our unhappiness. Yet it is an enlightening tool when we use it to aid us in seeing issues of control, fear, and martyrdom. This step creates a commonality between staff and management alike: we all created this discomfort, and we are all willing to be responsible for our actions.

Step 5: "We admitted to ourselves and to another human being the exact nature of our sabotaging behavior on the job." After writing a moral inventory in the previous step, we tell another person - - often our sponsor - - what is behind our destructive behavior. Fear is the essence of all destructive behavior. In telling our story, the issues that were so powerful that we felt we had to hide them will lose their power. When we admit our fears and open ourselves to healing, the fears will begin to dissipate. Admitting our fears of not knowing the answers, for example, allows us to see our patterns of self-criticism and self-judgement. We can then stop putting pressure on ourselves to know everything. We realize that the more knowledge anyone acquires, the more there is to learn, and the world of education becomes fresh and alive once we open ourselves to listening and learning.

Step 6: "We were entirely ready to listen to the guidance and, for a moment, to let go of our original viewpoint." Here is where we release rigid thinking and allow new ideas to manifest. Managers become willing to listen to staff, and staff become eager to hear new ideas.

Step 7: "Acknowledged the guidance, summarized it; asked questions to further understand it; said 'thank you' and agreed to undertake the suggestion." This is our opportunity to have our shortcomings removed as we move our egos out of the way. We become less defensive, and we co-create in an ambiance of cooperation. We see that many opinions and ideas can exist in the same space. Self-esteem of the corporation will climb as employees feel listened to and respected for their input.

Step 8: "Made a list of all the persons we had harmed and became willing to make amends to them, to others or to the corporation." When Deborah, a critical care nurse, admitted that she had sabotaged the graduate nurses from learning new skills by insisting on personally taking the most critical patients, she released herself from the expectation of being the most perfect nurse.

Step 9: "Made direct amends to such people whenever possible except when to do so would injure them or others." Deborah courageously apologized to the graduate nurses and volunteered to help them care for a critical patient. Through letting go of her need for control, Deborah received the gift of teaching and participating in these new nurses' learning process. She again felt the joy of her knowledge and her capabilities.

Step 10: "Continued to take personal inventory and when we were wrong promptly admitted it." This step is essential to prevent slipping back into old dysfunctional behaviors. Deborah will continue to monitor herself for issues of control and perfectionism.

Step 11: "We are now safe to let our entrepreneurial spirit come back to life." Anne Wilson Schaef explains that one of the characteristics of an addictive society is nonliving. When we again feel the enthusiasm for our work, we experience the entrepreneurial spirit coming back to life. We know that we are alive when we can again feel joy, sadness, excitement, and vulnerability.

Step 12: "Having recaptured our entrepreneurial spirit, we carried this message to others whom we saw imprisoned in resistance to their own productiveness and creativity." We do not all recover at the same time or in the same manner. Knowing this is a lesson in releasing control. We cannot make others work their program our way. We can only demonstrate what has worked for us. We must let go of our expectations of others. A way to check our own recovery from codependency is to ask,

"Am I able to stay on my own side of the street, or am I tempted to jump across my own and others' boundaries and try to fix the person who is recovering at a slower pace or in a different way?" Patience, kindness, and tolerance are required, as well as sharing our experience, strength, and hope.

Employee Assistance Programs

It is valuable to educate the employee assistance department in the twelve steps before introducing the program to the employees. When the program is initiated, employees who are already in recovery might be invited to speak to groups and to be available as sponsors if they so desire (their anonymity must be respected).

Outside Consultants

Outside consultants are useful to help facilitate groups and to guide employees through the steps. They, too, must be aware of their own codependent tendencies. If they are in a recovery program, they will more likely be able to maintain their own feelings and remain neutral.

REWARDS OF A HEALTHY INSTITUTION

A healthy institution is made up of healthy individuals. A healthy institution is possible as long as the individual staff and the administration work together to uncover any dysfunction and consequently to recover from the patterns of addiction and codependency. Although the twelve steps have been proven to be an effective program of recovery, there are other programs. Group support is an imperative component of any recovery program. Safety for those willing to share their experience, strength, and hope is essential. Where there is no shaming for vulnerabilty, the institution will benefit by becoming vulnerable enough to ask for help, for it is in the asking that recovery is possible.

When a healing institution commits to its own healing process, all kinds of rewards are reaped. Recovery is ongoing, reducing the potential for relapse and burnout among employees. Management is moral and flexible and welcomes challenge. The institution provides a safe and supportive environment for its staff as well as for its patients and visitors. The quality of the institution's service increases. The ultimate reward goes to those who come to the institution for healing, since the employees, by being allowed to heal, then, become authentic healers.

CHAPTER NINE

AUTHENTIC NURSING SERVICE:
TO THINE OWN SELF BE TRUE

If I can stop one heart from breaking,
I shall not live in vain;
If I can ease one life from aching, or cool one pain,
or help one fainting robin into his nest again,
I shall not live in vain.
- Emily Dickinson

Following a lecture I presented at a college of nursing, a student nurse asked if I recognized her. I did not. The student nurse quietly began to explain our connection. Some years before, I had been working in an intensive care unit where her husband was a patient suffering from sepsis as a result of pneumonia. The woman's husband had been on a ventilator for several weeks and had lapsed into a coma. He had suffered brain damage, and his prognosis was critical.

This student nurse explained to me how I was present for her personal grieving process. She talked to me about my tender touch when I cared for her husband. She recalled how much respect I had shown for his dignity. She told me how I had held her while she cried as they disconnected her husband from the life support machines. She said that she kept a letter I had written to her describing my personal feelings about the experience of death.

This woman was in nursing school now because she had been touched by a moment of authentic service. This moment was an expression of love. It had been a time of unity, a time of sharing the experience of life and death as equal participants. It was caring *with* rather than caring *for* . This is an example of that precious moment of authentic service that all nurses know. It is what makes nursing truly essential and needed.

Just what do we mean by authentic service? Let's first define service, then review dysfunctional service, and conclude with a discussion of authentic service.

The definition of service is threefold. First, service is the contribution to the welfare of others. The concern for the welfare of others is inherent in nursing. Yet how does one make such a contribution without causing others to become needy and dependent on the caregiver?

Second, service is useful labor that does not produce a tangible commodity. One cannot see or measure service. Although attempts have been made to measure the quality of nursing care through acuity studies and analytical tools, the spirit of service is invisible.

Third, service is a meeting of worship. It is the place to which we come unto another for the purpose of worshipping human life. Authentic service occurs when two or more gather as equals to care *with* rather than to care *for* one another, to worship life.

DYSFUNCTIONAL SERVICE

To understand the meaning of dysfunctional service, we need to first review the term *dysfunctional*. Very simply, it means it doesn't work. A dysfunctional family is one in which no one's needs are being met because, according to Carla Perez, the "parents (are) emotionally, chemically... or physically unavailable.... the family focus (is) somewhere else, not on us" (1991).

Since our needs are not being met, we learn to focus on meeting the needs of those around us. Since we are not being taken care of, we learn to take care of others as a way to take care of our own needs. We learn to take care of others to receive approval both from those we take care of and from the significant adults in our lives. We learn to take care of others so that we can feel like we count, that we matter. We get our sense of worth by helping others. Some of us carry our caretaking behaviors into our careers.

I learned dysfunctional service at a young age. I could take care of everyone else, since my focus was on everyone but myself. If you were in pain, I was uncomfortable. Therefore, I tried to fix you. I was so tuned in to others' pain that fixing came naturally to me. I was a great server. I believed I was serving authentically because it felt so natural. But the natural need to fix was a result of my inability to separate my pain from yours.

I served for many dysfunctional reasons. I served so that you would like me. I became a nurse so that I could look at your problems instead of my own. I served so that I could feel in control. If not in control, I felt an inner anxiety that stemmed from my uncontrollable past. I served so that I could feel needed, since I needed to be needed. I served so that you would give me esteem, because I could not give myself any. Dysfunctional service, then, is outer focused. Its goal is to look good in the name of service.

TRAITS OF DYSFUNCTIONAL SERVERS

As previously mentioned, people who grow up in dysfunctional families learn early to take care of others. Caretaking behaviors learned in early childhood manifest in many ways, the most predominant of which are control, guilt, low self-esteem, isolation, and pity.

Control

When I reach out to help you in an attempt to control, I am assuming a role of superiority, which puts you in an inferior role. I am the helper, you are helpless. I am needless, you are needy. If I keep you needy, I will feel in control. Since I will not allow you to be in control, you will learn that I will always do it for you. I have therefore done you a DISSERVICE disguised as SERVICE.

Guilt

"Dysfunctionality in a family sets up shoulds, oughts and musts by which each member is measured.... In such an environment, (our) natural powers are continuously discounted and judged as unacceptable" (Bradshaw, 1988:65-66). This sets us up to act out of guilt and an overdeveloped sense of responsibility for others.

If I've been taught to feel guilty when I take time for myself, I then believe that I *should* be helping more, I *ought* to take on one more committee, I *must* help one more patient even though my shift is over, or I *should* help a family member even though I am tired. I *must* keep serving and smiling even though I'm exhausted and on the verge of tears.

If I have feelings of guilt, I may try to absolve my sins through serving others rather than looking inward at why I feel guilty. Because I feel guilty when I am not serving, I take responsibility for others. When I do so, I am depriving them from learning their own lessons and from taking responsibility for their own lives.

Esteem

In dysfunctional service, self-esteem is replaced by other-esteem. My concept of myself is based on what others think of me or how much I can create dependent relationships. The problem with other-esteem is that if I look to others for approval and status, if I see myself through others' eyes and then others change their mind about how they view me, I will have to change my opinion of myself, adjusting to their perception of me. If my self-image is based on their image of me, I am vulnerable to sudden changes in my self-esteem.

Isolation

If I feel different from others, and if I can make others the patients and myself the helper, I can avoid feeling vulnerable. I can isolate myself in the many tasks of the helper in order to avoid true intimacy. These feelings of separation will limit what I have to offer. I must be able to experience the commonality that happens in authentic service so that I can experience intimacy and compassion.

Pity

The Zen Buddhists call pity "idiot compassion." Pity is observing an intoxicated man lying in the gutter, scooping him up, and taking him home to fix him, making him ready for a new life. Pity distracts people from feeling their pain — and it is done in the name of kindness. It is based on our own discomfort with the suffering of another, taking care of others even when they have not asked for our help. We enter uninvited into their territory, fixing and serving them, with no idea of the lessons that they are trying to learn through their suffering. Pity is an obstacle we impose on another's growth. It is other oriented and is based on relieving our own guilt. Pity is self-serving. It is not meant to esteem another; it esteems self through seeing the other in a pitiful state.

AUTHENTIC SERVICE

Unlike dysfunctional service, which is controlled, authentic service is spontaneous. It comes from the heart, not from the mind. It is based on love and compassion, not on fear. It is its own reward. Before we can engage in authentic service, however, we need to become authentic human beings. To do this, we must first look within ourselves.

Developmental Stages of the Authentic Self
Jacquelyn Small (1991) defines three developmental stages of the authentic Self. Each one is important for reaching the place where we can serve from our authenticity.

The first stage of human development is *selfishness* . In this formative stage, the child develops a sense of self-importance. The child needs to be validated by focusing on self. If we have never been given a chance to focus on self, this task may still be awaiting us, for it is only when a person becomes satisfied with self that he or she can move on to the second stage. There is a judgement placed on selfishness, yet we need to come to service with a full cup of self so as not to become drained.

The second stage of authenticity is that of developing a sense of *selfness*. Here is where we progress from self-centeredness to self-knowingness. "To thine own self be true" is the motto of this stage. We look at our weaknesses and our strengths, and we discover what we have to offer. We explore our talents and interests and determine what type of service we want to pursue. We learn our limitations as well as the warning signs of when we may be giving too much or for the wrong reasons.

Self-awareness must accompany the commitment to serve, or the danger of addictive caretaking replacing authentic service will be present. When we move into our authenticity, we can serve from self-esteem, which Pia Mellody defines as "the internal experience of one's own preciousness and value" (1989:7). Self-esteem is different from self-importance in that it is based on humility, a humble knowingness, and love of self.

The third stage of the authentic self is *selflessness*. Dogen Zenji explains, "To study the Way is to study the Self. To study the Self is to forget the Self. To forget the Self is to be enlightened by all things. To be enlightened by all things is to remove the barrier between Self and Other" Ram Dass & Gorman, (1985:42). Here, the three stages of self investigation — selfishness, selfness, and selflessness — bring us to the way, and the way is authentic service.

Traits of Authentic Servers

Authentic servers possess the same attributes that one will observe in the self-actualized individual. These attributes include compassion, humility, love and joy, and true selflessness.

Compassion

Compassion is based on love. Compassion may be walking by the intoxicated man in the gutter, feeling humility, saying with all of our heart, "There, but for the grace of God, go I," and silently thanking him. Compassion is buying the same man a sandwich and taking it to him in the gutter. It is helping him find an AA meeting if he asks for help. Compassion is the act of suffering *with* rather than suffering *for*. Compassion is allowing ourselves to be vulnerable to another's suffering yet not becoming enmeshed in it.

Pity is caring for. Compassion is caring with. Pity is a trait of the caretaker; compassion, of the caregiver. How does one move beyond pity, beyond serving from the ego, beyond serving as the helper who gets esteemed by helping? How does one keep from feeling selfish and guilty when allowing the intoxicated man to remain in the gutter? By healing ourselves, we will know the authentic way to help others to heal themselves.

Humility

Mother Teresa of Calcutta teaches, "We must accept our vulnerability and limitations in regard to others. This is essential in gaining their confidence. We cannot expect to help others from the outside" (Barbier,1982:12). She explains that it takes humility to acknowledge one's limitations, one's helplessness, or one's inadequacy. A humble nurse may be seen walking into a terminally ill patient's room, sitting down next to the patient, allowing herself to cry, and saying, "I feel frightened by your pain. If I do not admit that to myself, I might become phony, hardened, or shallow. That might interfere with your care. Please help me understand how I can help so that my fear doesn't hinder my service."

Love and Joy

In her book *The Search for the Beloved*, Jean Houston tells of her personal encounter with Mother Teresa. When she met her at a conference, Jean asked her how she could do so much and always remain in a state of joy.

"My dear," Mother Teresa answered, "it is because I am so deeply in love. I am so in a state of love that I see the face of my Beloved in the face of the dying man in the streets of Calcutta. I see my Beloved in the day-old child who's left outside our convent, and in the leper whose flesh is decaying; and I can't do enough for my Beloved! That is why I try to do something beautiful for God" (Houston, 1987:134).

True Selflessness

Unselfish love is the spiritual motivation embraced by those who choose a path committed to the service of others. True selflessness is not the abandonment of self, but rather the surrender of selfish motives. The result of this surrender is self love, or self-esteem. We experience our preciousness and value and reach out from that centered place of love, serving authentically.

Recognizing Authentic Service

What does authentic service feel like? How will we know that we are being authentic servers? When we are practicing authentic service, we will serve from our unique selves. We will serve lovingly. Because fear and love cannot exist in the same space, we will be less fearful and we will be able to love our patients. We will also be able to love ourselves enough to know when we need personal nurturing. We will know how to receive as well as how to give.

We will enter a healing relationship with those we serve. We will share intimacy and admit to our vulnerabilities. We will eliminate the arrogance of the unhealthy helper. We will release control and know that we too are in need of healing. When we heal our own wounds, we will cease projecting personal discomfort, trying to fix this same discomfort in our patients. We will know that to be healers, we must first be healed.

We will know our special contributions as well as our personal limitations. We will know the joy of service. We will support our peers rather than compete for approval and acknowledgement. We will provide support for the spiritual, mental, emotional, and physical growth of those who are assigned to our care.

Authentic service can be seen in the nurse who has nurtured herself, the healer who has been healed. It is the service we hear when the nurse can speak from her heart to the patient these simple and humble words, "I am here. Let's heal together."

Rewards of Authentic Service

"The reward, the real grace, of conscious service... is the opportunity not only to help relieve suffering but to grow in wisdom, experience greater unity, and have a good time while we're doing it" (Ram Dass & Gorman, 1985:16).

The reward of authentic service is self-growth. Authentic service originates from that part of one's being that seeks evolution. Authentic service is unconditional. It happens when one is acting out of responsibility — the ability to respond. It happens when one is esteeming oneself and not searching for esteem from others.

Patricia Donahue writes about her concepts of the true rewards of nursing:

> The look of incredible joy on the faces of new parents as you place the newborn baby in their arms. The feel of a child's arms around your neck as he hugs you tightly, knowing and trusting that you will protect him. The touch of a patient's fingers on your cheek when the patient cannot verbally communicate but wishes to say "Thank you." The closeness that you share with a family of a terminally ill patient. Eyes that light up in recognition of your presence. The peace and contentment that are experienced as you sit and hold the hand of one who is dying. The knowledge that you have truly cared 'for' and 'about' another individual. The satisfaction of assisting an individual to achieve under the most bleak of circumstances. The smile of a patient when he is told that he does not have cancer (1989, preface).

As nurses, we are blessed with seeing people get well. We are given opportunities to relate to others in a meaningful manner, where facades fade away and are replaced by intimacy and where our egos do not take credit and we can participate in the healing process. We may see our patients walk out the door with more independence than when they arrived. We may receive the blessings of helping a terminal patient pass on. These rewards bring validation to our spiritual beliefs.

Picture a patient who enters the doors of a hospital that is based on authentic service. The patient is in need of healing both the mind and the body. Upon entering, the patient is greeted by a nurse who is knowledgeable about recovery because she has personally experienced it. As the patient participates in the nursing assessment, the nurse asks him about the kind of recovery he would like to be involved in. The nurse takes her time with the patient, for she knows that this is the most important contact this patient will have throughout his stay.

This story goes on, perhaps a vision of nurses moving from dysfunctional to authentic service. What would it look like if nurses healed themselves and their profession? This vision is the gift of recovery, the very image of authentic nursing service.

INDEX

REFERENCES

Ackerman, Robert J. *Perfect Daughters*. Deerfield Beach, FL: Health Communications,1989.

Alcoholics Anonymous. Third Edition. New York: AA World Services, 1976.

American Psychiatric Association. *Let's Talk Facts About Post-Traumatic Stress Disorder*, 1988.

Barbier, Jean, & Gorree, Georges. *The Love of Christ: Mother Teresa of Calcutta*. San Francisco: Harper & Row, 1982.

Beattie, Melody. *Codependent No More: How to Stop Controlling Others & Start Caring for Yourself.* San Francisco: Harper & Row, 1987.

Berry, Carmen Renee. *When Helping You Is Hurting Me*. San Francisco: Harper & Row, 1988.

Bissel, LeClair, & Haberman, Paul W. *Alcoholism in the Professions*. New York: Oxford University Press, 1984.

Black, Claudia. *It Will Never Happen To Me*. Denver, CO: Medical Administration Company, 1981.

Bower, Fay L. "Shared Governance: A Professional Model for Nursing Practice." *California Nursing.* Nov./Dec. 1990, pp. 29 - 32.

Bower, Fay L. "Shared Governance, Part II: The Early Implementation Phase." *California Nursing.* Jan/Feb. 1991, pp. 25 - 27.

Board of Registered Nursing, State of California. "Diversion Regulations" Authority cited: Business & Professions Code Sections 2715, 2770.7, Reference. Business & Professions Code Section 2770.7.

Board of Registered Nursing, State of California. "Registered Nurses in Recovery: Diversion Program. (Pamphlet). No date listed.

Bradshaw, John. *Bradshaw On: The Family*. Deerfield Beach, FL: Health Communications, 1988.

Buxton, Millicent E. & Jessup, Marty. "Statement of the Problem." Bay Area Taskforce for Impaired Nurses, Haight Ashbury Training and Education Project, San Francisco, CA, 1984.

California Nurses Association. "Resolution on Chemical Dependency Among Nurses." Approved by the 1983 House of Delegates, March 7, 1983.

Crosby, Linda and Bissell, LeClair. *Enabling in the Health Professions*. Minneapolis, MN. The Johnson Institute. 1991.

Donahue, Patricia M. Ph.D, RN. *Nursing, The Finest Art*. St. Louis. C. V. Mosby Co. 1989.

Duerk, Judith. *Circle of Stones*. San Diego, CA: LuraMedia, 1989.

Guggenbuhl - Craig, Adolf. *Power in the Helping Professions*. Dallas, TX. Spring Publications, Inc. 1971.

Hall, Sarah F., & Wray, Linda M. "Codependency: Nurses Who Give Too Much." *American Journal of Nursing*, July 1990.

Houston, Jean. *The Search for the Beloved: Journeys in Mythology and Sacred Psychology*. Los Angeles, Jeremy P. Tarcher, 1987.

Jefferson, Linda V., "Help for the Helper." *American Journal of Nurses*, 1982.

King, Laurel. *Women of Power*. Berkeley. Celestial Arts, 1989.

Lerner, Harriet Goldhor, PhD. *The Dance of Anger.* New York: Harper & Row, 1985.

Marcus, Mary. "Who Heals the Healer?" *Readings in Psychosynthesis: Volume 2.* Department of Applied Psychology/ Ontario Institute for Studies in Education, Toronto, 1988.

Mellody, Pia. *Facing Codependence.* San Francisco: Harper & Row. 1989.

Milkman, Harvey and Shaeffer, Howard J. *The Addictions: Multidiscipinary Perspectives and Treatment.* "Treatment of the Chemical Dependent Health Profession." Buxton, Millicent E. & Jessup, Marty & Landry, Mim J. Lexington Books. Lexington, Mass. 1985.

Morse, RM. Martin, MA. Swenson, WM. and Niven, RG. "Prognosis of Physician Treatment for Alcoholism and Drug Dependency." *Journal of American Medical Association.* Issue 251, Vol. 6.

Patten, Tomas. Personal Interview: "PTSD: A Delayed Stress Syndrome in the Vietnam Vet." 1985.

Perez, Carla. *Getting Off the Merry-Go-Round.* New York: Simon & Schuster, 1991.

Ram Dass & Gorman, Paul. *How Can I Help?* New York. Alfred A. Knopf. 1985.

Riley, Mary. *Corporate Healing: Solutions to the Impact of the Addictive Personality in the Workplace.* Deerfield Beach, FL: Health Communications, 1990.

Riso, Don Richard. *Personality Types: Using the Enneagram for Self-Discovery.* Boston. Houghton Mifflin, 1987.

Robbins, Collette E. "A Monitored Treatment Program for Impaired Health Care Professionals." *Journal of Nursing*

Administration, Feb. 1987, pp. 17-21.

Rubin, JoAnne. "Critical Incident Stress Debriefing: Helping the Helper." *Journal of Emergency Nursing.* Vol. 16, No. 4. July/Aug. 1990.

Schaef, Anne Wilson. *When Society Becomes an Addict.* San Francisco: Harper & Row, 1987.

Schaef, Anne Wilson, & Fassel, Diane.*The Addictive Organization.* San Francisco: Harper & Row, 1988.

Small, Jacquelyn. *Awakening in Time: The Journey from Co-depencence to Co-creation.* Bantam. July 1991.

Snow, Candace & Willard, David. *I'm Dying to Take Care of You.* Redmond, WA. Professional Counselor Books. 1989.

Subby, Robert. *Co-Dependency, an Emerging Issue.* Pampano Beach, FL. Health Communications, 1984.

Summers, Caryn. *Circle of Health: Recovery Through the Medicine Wheel.* Freedom, CA: Crossing Press. 1991.

Tanner, Wilda B. *The Mystical Magical Marvelous World of Dreams.* Tahiequah, OK: Sparrow Hawk Press. 1988.

Tyrell, Mary M. "The Unseen Veteran." *VA Practitioner*, Oct. 1987.

Ward, Patrick, Eck, Catherine, & Sanguino, Thomas. "Emergency Nursing at the Epicenter: The Loma Prieta Earthquake." *Journal of Emergency Nursing,* July/Aug 1990, pp. 49A - 55A.

Whitfield, Charles L. *Healing the Child Within.* Deerfield Beach, FL: Health Communications, 1989.

Woititz, Janet G. Ed.D. *The Self-Sabotage Syndrome: Adult*

Children in the Workplace. Deerfield Beach, FL: Health Communications, 1989.

Zukav, Gary. *The Seat of the Soul.* New York: Simon & Schuster, 1989.

ADDITIONAL SUGGESTED READING

Beattie, Melody. *Beyond Codependency.* San Francisco: Harper & Row, 1989.

Beattie, Melody. *Codependent No More.* New York: Harper/Hazelden, 1987.

Becker, Robert. *Addicted to Misery. The Other Side of Codependency.* Deerfield Beacy, FL: Health Communications, 1989.

Black, Claudia. *It Will Never Happen To Me.* New York: Ballentine Books, 1981.

Blume, Sheila B. *Alcohol/Drug Dependent Women: New Insights into Their Special Problems, Treatment, Recovery.* Minneapolis. Johnson Institute. 1988.

Bowden, Julie, and Gravitz, Herbert. *Genesis: Spirituality in Recovery from Childhood Traumas.* Pompano Beach, FL: Health Communications, 1988.

Carlson, Richard, & Shielf, Benjamin. *Healers on Healing.* Los Angeles: Jeremy P. Tarcher, 1989.

Chopich, Erika J., and Paul, Margaret. *Healing Your Aloneness.* San Francisco: Harper & Row, 1990.

Church, Dawson, and Sherr, Alan. *The Heart of the Healer.* New York: Aslan Publishing, 1987.

Crosby, Linda R., and Bissell, LeClair. *To Care Enough:*

Intervention with Chemically Dependent Colleagues. Minneapolis: Johnson Institute, 1989.

Ehrenreich, Barbara, & English, Deirdre. *Witches, Midwives, and Nurses: A History of Women Healers.* New York: The Feminist Press, 1973.

Gil, Eliana. *Outgrowing the Pain.* Walnut Creek, CA: Launch Press, 1983.

Gravitz, Herbert L., & Bowden, Julie D. *Recovery: A Guide for Adult Children of Alcoholics.* New York: Simon & Schuster, 1985.

Hardy, Jean. *A Psychology With A Soul.* England: Arkana, 1987.

How to Use Intervention in Your Professional Practice. Minneapolis: Johnson Institute, 1987.

Kraegel, Janet & Kachoyeanos, Mary. *Just A Nurse.* New York: Dell Publishing, 1989.

Kritsberg, W. *The Adult Children of Alcoholics Syndrome: From Discovery to Recovery.* Pompano Beach, FL: Health Communications, 1986.

Lee, John. "What To Do About Your Anger and Grief." In Lee, John, with Bill Stott, *Recovery: Plain and Simple.* Deerfield Beach, FL: Health Communications, 1990.

Madow, Leo. *Anger — How to Recognize and Cope With It.* New York: Charles Scribner's Sons, 1972.

Nightingale, Florence. *Cassandra.* New York: The Feminist Press, 1979.

Peck, M.Scott. *The Road Less Traveled.* New York: Simon & Shuster. 1978.

Phelps, Stanlee & Austin, Nancy. *The Assertive Woman: A New*

Look. San Luis Obispo, CA: Impact Publishers, 1987.

Rosellini, Gayle, and Worden, Mark. *Of Course You're Angry*. San Francisco: Harper/Hazelden, 1985.

Vicinus, Martha, & Newgaard, Bea. *Ever Yours, Florence Nightingale*. Cambridge, MA: Harvard University Press, 1990.

Viscott, David. *The Language of Feelings*. New York: Pocket Books, 1976.

Wegscheider - Cruse, Sharon. *Choice-Making*. Pompano Beach, FL: Health Communications, 1985.

Woititz, Janet Geringer. *Adult Children of Alcoholics*. Pompano Beach, FL: Health Communications, 1983.

Zweig, Connie. *To Be A Woman*. Los Angeles: Jeremy P. Tarcher, 1990.

ABOUT THE AUTHOR

Caryn Summers worked in managerial roles within the nursing profession for many years. She is now a writer and public speaker, presenting workshops for nurses and helping professionals on codependency, chemical dependency, institutional cobehavior, recovery, and authentic nursing service. She is being received in colleges, hospitals, and private organizations.

Caryn works with the California Board of Registered Nurses' Diversion Program, providing assessment and intervention for chemically impaired nurses in Northern California. She facilitates a nurse support group and provides private consultation to hospitals, employee assistance programs, and nursing staffs who are challenged with healing addictions and dysfunctional behavior patterns.

In her first book, entitled *Circle of Health: Recovery through the Medicine Wheel,* Caryn provides creative tools for recovery from codependency and other process addictions. This workbook traces a path of self-awareness using symbols, traditions, mythology, Jungian psychology, and psychosynthesis. Caryn conducts circle workshops for the audience who is interested in creative recovery. She believes that the recovery process can be imaginative and exciting and utilizes mythology, symbolism, and imagination in her work.

Among her personal interests, Caryn enjoys growing and drying herbs, backpacking, tennis, aerobics, running, journal writing, weaving and spinning: "I find that spinning becomes my meditation and is a wonderful access into the world of mythology. As I spin the wool, I spin tales of growth and empowerment."

For more information, contact the author through:
Commune - A - Key Publishing and Education
P O Box 507
Mt. Shasta, CA 96067
(916) 926-6305

ORDER FORM

Need a copy for a friend? You may order directly.

Caregiver, Caretaker (From Dysfunctional to Authentic Service in Nursing).

Also available by Caryn Summers:

Circle of Health: Recovery Through the Medicine Wheel.
"Recovery means the regaining of self, the person we started out to be. This workbook combines art, mythology, symbols, native American tradition and psychology with the tools practiced in many twelve-step recovery programs."

Mail this form with your check or money order payable to:
    Commune-A-Key Publishing
    P O Box 507B
    Mt. Shasta, CA 96067

Caregiver, Caretaker	$16.95 each	$_____
Circle of Health.	$12.95 each	$_____
California residents add 7.25% sales tax		$_____
Shipping and handling: $3.00 first book, $1.25 each additional		$_____
Total $ enclosed		$_____

Name _____

Address _____

City _____ State _____ Zip_____

_____ Please send me information on tapes and future publications.